EDICIONES
FUNDACION ANTORCHAS 1989

The author and the Fundación Antorchas would like to thank all those who have helped in the publication of this book, especially those descendents of early settlers in Bariloche who provided many of the photographs and a considerable amount of information. A complete list of names is not possible for reasons of space –and the fear of inevitable omissions– but our gratitude to them is in no way diminished.

Text and selection of photographs: Ricardo Vallmitjana
Introductory essay: Edgardo Krebs
Graphic design: Carlos Montanari
Cover: Oscar Pintor
Map artwork: Rodolfo Camacho
Translation into English: Martin Eayrs
General supervision: Mario Valledor

Printed and bound by
Gaglianone Establecimiento Gráfico S.A.,
Buenos Aires, Argentina

Queda hecho el depósito que marca la ley 11.123

Impreso en Argentina
Printed in Argentina

I.S.B.N. 950-9837-01-6 (English language)
I.S.B.N. 950-9837-02-4 (idioma castellano)

RICARDO VALLMITJANA

BARILOCHE, MY HOME

Foreword

THESE photographs, painstakingly collected over the years by Ricardo Vallmitjana, help us to rebuild in our imagination the past of the town and region of Bariloche, a past which, if perhaps uninspired, has with the passing of time been embellished with adventure, legend and fantasy.

Alongside these vivid images of the everyday history of the town and its environs, the freshness and spontaneity of the text which accompanies the photos permits us a glimpse of some intimate moments of this pioneer Patagonian community. At the same time Edgardo Krebs' introductory essay, perhaps written with a certain nostalgia in moments he could spare from more time-absorbing commitments at Oxford, demonstrates the mysterious ways in which harsh and occasionally vulgar reality can be transformed into illusion or phantasmagoric poetry.

This collection of photographs is being published by the Fundación Antorchas –as was an earlier one dedicated to the work of the photographer Fernando Paillet and his testimony to life in the *pampa gringa** at the beginning of the century[1]– as part of its desire to keep the past, which is part of our common national heritage, from vanishing forever.

The photographs in this book have neither the photographic merit of Paillet's studies nor the technical quality which can be achieved through enlargements of glass plate negatives. Here we have a case of documentary rather than artistic photography; of social rather than photographic history (although some of the photographs in the following pages may well be deemed to have artistic merit), and we should in any case remember that the modest snapshots which help us to preserve our memories are just as much part of our photographic past as other, more professional ones.

The town of Bariloche developed rather differently from most Argentine cities. Even for a country consisting mainly of European immigrants it was at first an amazing melting pot for settlers of different origins, different mother tongues, different communities, all striving to maintain their own cultural identity without fragmenting into hostile groups. Bariloche and the surrounding lands, with their temperate climate, their thickly forested, snow-capped mountains, their multitudinous lakes –so unlike the places where the majority of Argentines live– and their location beyond the desert** on the edge of Patagonia, were –in those not so distant days before highways and aeroplanes– almost as remote as the far side of the moon.

Today Bariloche is nearer to the everyday experience of those who live in other parts of the country; to those who live, to use the Patagonian phrase, in the "north". Nevertheless, for reasons which go further than mere latitude, Bariloche continues to be the "south". Perhaps this book will help us to understand better why this should be, and will permit the men and women of the north to come nearer to the south, to the cold, to the Cordillera; to come nearer to Patagonia.

---

* The fertile pampa plains were cattle and sheep raising country until, around 1870, European immigrants began growing grain crops. The agricultural farms and the newly arrived settlers –called *gringos* by the natives– changed the physical and social landscape. The area where this happened, mainly the hinterland of the city of Rosario, became known as the *pampa gringa*.

[1] Fernando Paillet, *Fotografías 1894-1940*. Ediciones Fundación Antorchas, 1987.

** The semi-arid regions between the Argentine pampas and the Andes were usually referred to in the 19th century as the "desert", a name which, if perhaps misleading, fired the country's imagination. Thus when the troops of Buenos Aires drove inland in the late 1870s to subdue the Indians it was said –and it is recorded thus in history– that they "conquered the desert". The Andes and Nahuel Huapi campaigns, mentioned below, were part of these military operations.

"Nowhere is a place"

I

"Imagination is the thing, I should say. It's far more important than physical courage." Jorge Luis Borges[1]

"The imagination nourishes man and causes him to act. It is a collective, social, and historical phenomenon. A history without the imagination is a mutilated, disembodied history." Jacques Le Goff [2]

MIRRORS always worried Borges. In one of his poems, he refers to mirrors *"lying in wait for unsuspecting passersby"*. In "The Veiled Mirrors"[3] he is more explicit: *"As a child I was aware of the horrors of a ghostly duplication or multiplication of reality (...) when faced by large mirrors. The way they functioned permanently and infallibly, the way they followed me and my movements whatsoever I might do, their cosmic pantomime; these became supernatural as night drew in (...) I know I used to keep an uneasy eye on them"*.

Photographs also multiply reality, and they too have a certain permanence and infallibility, but their cosmic pantomime is fragmentary. The fact that they reproduce only fragments, although perhaps less odious than the mirrors' relentless ambush, is disturbing in its own way. A photograph never tells the whole story –that has to be repieced by the viewer. The information crystallized in the fragment is merely a starting point. As with Heraclitus and his river, one never goes twice to the same collection of photographs, for with the passing of time the value of the images and the way one appreciates them both change, as do the viewer and his way of interacting with the photographs. They multiply reality less passively than Borges' mirrors, because they need someone to set them in motion.

It is fitting that the photographs within this book should be set against the sparse yet strong iconographic Patagonian tradition of the partly mythical, partly real region to which Bariloche belongs. The portraits of Carlos Wiederhold and the Texan cowboy Jarred Jones are merely an extension of the chronological sequence which includes the fantastic prints collected by Theodor De Bry in his "Great Journeys" (1590-1634), and the impossibly tall natives who grace the pages of Captain Byron's narrative[4].

Things fantastic are so real in Patagonia that any intrusion of genuine reality seems out of place. *"Patagonia has not been widely photographed"*, writes Paul Theroux[5]. *"I had no mental image of it, only the fanciful blur of legend (...) And when, after a long trip, I arrived in Patagonia I felt I was nowhere. But the most surprising thing of all was that I was still in the world –I had been travelling south for months. The landscape was a gaunt expression, but I could not deny that it had readable features and that I existed in it. This was a discovery –the look of it. I thought: 'Nowhere is a place'."*

Confusion and surprise are part and parcel of the New World. Christopher Columbus died firm in the belief that he had reached the East by way of a non-African route. Americo Vespucci, a friend of Columbus and leading navigator of the Casa de Indias from 1508 onwards, had already written his famous "Mundus Novus" letter to his patron Lorenzo de Medici in 1504, on the strength of two or more voyages across the Atlantic. Vespucci returned from his first voyage to the Americas (1499-1500) believing that the Orinoco and Amazon deltas formed part of the South-Asian coastline. Only after his second voyage in 1501, in which he sailed South at least as far as the

[1] *In Memory of Borges.* Edited and with an Introduction by Norman Thomas Di Giovanni. Constable, London, 1989.

[2] Jacques Le Goff. *The Medieval Imagination.* University of Chicago Press, 1988.

[3] Jorge Luis Borges. *El Hacedor.* In "Obras Completas". Emecé, Buenos Aires, 1974.

[4] Lord John Byron. *Journey Around the World, 1764-1765.*

[5] Bruce Chatwin and Paul Theroux. *Patagonia Revisited.* Houghton Mifflin, Boston, 1986.

River Plate and possibly to the Gulf of San Julián, did Vespucci realize that the lands he had explored constituted a genuine "new world".

The very name "America" was assigned almost arbitrarily by "a group of scholars living in the mountains of Lorraine"[6]. The cartographer Martin Waldseemüller, in the prologue to his "Cosmographiae Introductio" (1507), states, in what has come to be regarded as the birth certificate of the New World:

> But now these parts (Europe, Asia and Africa, the three continents of the Ptolomeic geography) have been extensively explored and a fourth part has been discovered by Americus Vespuccius, as will be seen in the appendix: I do not see what right any one would have to object to calling this part after Americus, who discovered it and who is a man of intelligence, and so to name it Amerige, that is, the Land of Americus, or America: since both Europe and Asia got their names from women[7].

Waldseemüller's depiction of America is hardly recognizable. Little more than a few rivers, more imagined than real, petering out into the empty white space beyond a narrow strip of known coastland. Indeed, the word "INCOGNITA" boldly adorns one side of the map.

For the historian Fernand Braudel, America is a European invention, "the achievement by which Europe most truly revealed her own nature"[8]. But this work, according to Braudel, took so long to complete that its meaning can only be comprehended if viewed in its entirety, that is if seen in terms of the complexity of its history.

The struggle for maritime control which set England, Spain and Portugal against each other forms part of that history. So do the ambitions of Kings, Courts and fortune hunters, and so does the work of geographers and scholars such as Richard Hakluyt, less interested in understanding the New World than in turning it to his own advantage in order to "make England economically independent of Europe"[9].

Prisoners who might otherwise have died in their cells were launched into the unknown, trapped in the tiny world of tiny boats, at the mercy of merciless sea-captains. These were the men that "only an angel could satisfy". We know of at least one of these that he boarded ship with a box containing a chirping cricket whose song would remind him of the land he was leaving behind[10].

In 1534 Charles V divided his new territories, several times larger than the whole of Europe, into four zones. The first of these he assigned to Francisco de Pizarro, the second to Almagro, the third to Pedro de Mendoza and the fourth, further south, to Simón de Alcazaba.

This simple division demonstrates how South America in a sense started out as the consequence of an arbitrary act. Perhaps it also helps to explain the extremes of solitude suffered by men such as Sarmiento de Gamboa on seas and unending plains ("... to die or do what he came to do, or not return to Spain nor to any place where people might ever see him")[11], and the mutinies faced by, amongst others, Magellan and Drake, and put down by "dismembering", "stabbing"[12], and "decapitation"[13].

This contrast between reality and fiction, between the New World as it really was, unexpectedly harsh, and as the imagination projected it, created a magic zone in which people like the conquistador Aguirre simply disappeared. So too did seekers of gold and lost cities, their expeditions in ruins and they themselves finally at

[6] Jonathan Cohen. *The Naming of America.* In *The American Voice*, Kentucky, N° 13, Winter 1988.

[7] *Ibid.*, p. 66.

[8] Fernand Braudel. *Civilization and Capitalism 15th – 18th Century.* Vol. III. The Perspective of the World. Collins, London, 1984.

[9] Jack Beeching. Introduction to: *Richard Hakluyt, Voyages and Discoveries.* Penguin Classics, 1987.

[10] Salvador de Madariaga. *Historia del muy magnífico señor don Cristóbal Colón.* Sudamericana, Buenos Aires. For a history of navigation in the South Atlantic from Magellan to the steam age, see Felix Riesenberg's *Cape Horn.*

[11] Pedro Sarmiento de Gamboa. *Viaje al estrecho de Magallanes en los años 1579 y 1580 y noticia de la expedición que después se hizo para poblarle.*

[12] Antonio de Pigafetta. *Primer viaje en torno del globo.*

[13] *Voyage of Francis Drake About the Whole Globe,* 1628.

one with the jungle or the plains they trod unseeingly.

"Whether it is a question of the geography of America, its flora and fauna, or the nature of its inhabitants" writes the historian J. H. Elliott[14], "the same kind of pattern seems constantly to recur in the European response. It is as if, at a certain point, the mental shutters come down; as if, with so much to see and absorb and understand, the effort suddenly becomes too much for them, and Europeans retreat to the half-light of their traditional mental world."

Vespucci's famous letters, considered apocryphal by some; the pictures collected by De Bry; the "Journeys and Discoveries" compiled by Hakluyt; these are just part of the troubled, semi-coherent collection of half truths alluding to and representing America. They also show through omission the latent force of an unspoken commentary; the power of silence.

When Pigafetta first described Patagonia, he could find no words in his dictionary to describe the fauna he saw. The "chingolos"* he called "sparrows", the penguins he saw were "geese", and as for the guanaco, it was "a commonly encountered animal with a mule's head and ears, a camel's body, a deer's legs and a horse's tail"[15].

Neither was he equipped to describe,

or even to understand, the man of "enormous stature" spotted one day "when we least expected it", almost naked, dancing and singing on the shore, and throwing sand up over his head[16].

The world in which Pigafetta lived and wrote was very different to ours. The sun moved around the earth, and in the European forests of the time encounters with elves and gnomes were a very real possibility. Mermaids sang by the seashores, unicorns pranced in the glades, and somewhere hidden away skulked that strange hybrid of lion with human head, the manticore.

And we should not treat such inventions lightly. T. H. White, translator into English of a Latin bestiary of the twelfth century, warns us: "The bestiary is a serious scientific work... a cameleopard is a genuine animal, and by no means a bad attempt to describe an unseen creature which was as big as a camel while being spotted as a leopard, i.e. a giraffe! (...) the real pleasure comes with identifying the existing creature, not with laughing at a supposedly imaginary one"[17].

Pigafetta, whose text begins the sequence continued in this book, was brief and concise in his impressions. We can see the animals he was trying to describe; can see a shaman in the man of "enormous stature" who

danced, sang and threw sand over his head. The missing pieces in the picture are clear and have been preserved intact. We can perhaps also understand this giant's behaviour and suggest an explanation for his actions: that he was not dancing in vain, rather he was trying to interpret the strange caravels that had entered his life in terms of the world which he knew and inhabited.

Other later chronicles were less faithful to reality than Pigafetta's, and enlarged the fantastic elements he only suggested. The Tehuelche Indians, for example, which he correctly describes as of above average height ("Among American Indians, the Tehuelche were probably the tallest")[18], reappear in later texts as almost monstrous giants.

Many of these texts were written by people who had never even been to Patagonia, but who were nevertheless collaborators in the construction of its myth, the myth of a place on the edge of the possible, "a pictorial and literary tradition lasting nearly 300 years"[19] (which continues still).

Patagonia has been described in Dutch, German, English, Polish, Finnish, and French; by seamen, scientists, and adventurers; and by people like Lady Dixie, an English aristrocrat who wanted to replace the world-weary view afforded her by a

[14] J. H. Elliott. *The Old World and the New.* Cambridge University Press, 1970.

* *Junco capensis*, the rufous-collared sparrow.

[15] Pigafetta, *op. cit.*

[16] *Ibid*, p. 14.

[17] T. H. White, *The Bestiary, A Book of Beasts.* Putnam's, New York, 1960.

[18] William Sturtevant. *Patagonian Giants and the Baroness Hyde de Nueville's Iroquois Drawings.* In *Ethnohistory*, 27.4.1982.

[19] William Sturtevant, *op. cit.*

London armchair with one from a saddle in the utterest ends of the earth.

And it has also been described by writers. Bruce Chatwin[20] discovered or invented —perhaps both— a literary ancestry for Patagonia, adding his name to those of Melville, Edgar Allan Poe, Dante, Shakespeare, Swift, Coleridge and others who had written about the region.

According to Chatwin, Dante, who "believed with the Greeks that the entire southern Hemisphere was uninhabited, uninhabitable and thus out of bounds for man", agrees with the European Renaissance poets, who "were soon busy weaving mythologies out of Magellan", "the trembling of the sea" and the deserted shores "that never saw any man". His list includes Góngora and John Donne.

For Melville, says Chatwin, Patagonia is "as an adjective for the outlandish, the monstrous and fatally attractive". Perhaps so. But in the case of Melville "the undeliverable, nameless perils of the whale" and the "marvels of a thousand Patagonian sights and sounds" are no excuse for amazing inventions or a purposeless story. They form part of an allegory, the background of which should be considered from an ethical point of view. Fantasy, strangeness, and fatal attraction lead Melville to reflect on man's destiny and his responsibility for his actions.

Similar echoes can be found in

Coleridge's magnificent poem "The Rime of the Ancient Mariner". The line "I shot the Albatross" finally releases the pent-up emotions of the mariner, haunted by the "fiends that plague" him because he had brought down with his bow the albatross which had followed his ship "in mist and cloud, on mast or shroud."

Chatwin points to Captain Shelvocke's book "A Voyage Around the World" (London, 1726) as Coleridge's source of inspiration, specifically to an episode which is mentioned as occurring off the shore of Tierra del Fuego. He also names Captain James Weddell's "Voyage towards the South Pole" as the inspiration for "Narrative of Arthur Gordon Pym of Nantucket", and goes on to find echoes of Poe's book in Dostoyevski, Baudelaire and Rimbaud.

Any region in the world could be proud of such a pedigree. But Chatwin had little interest in delving into the moral or reflective aspects of stories uprooted from the fantastic scenery of their Patagonian backcloth. He was more concerned with verifying the relationship between fatal attraction and literary imagination, and it is consistent with this aim that his Patagonia differs from the real one, or from that other one in which there are also people of flesh and bone, and in which there are towns like Bariloche. His Patagonia comes not from Tehuelche footprints in the sand, but from a chivalric tale, "Primaleón de Grecia" whose pages are terrorized by "the strange beast named Patagon".

Chatwin explains that this book was written anonymously and published in Spain in 1512, seven years before Magellan's journey. It was translated into English by Anthony Mundy, a friend of Shakespeare's, in 1596, fifteen years before the publication of "The Tempest". Chatwin supposes that both Magellan and Shakespeare would have read this book. According to Chatwin's theory, Magellan saw in the Tehuelches his monster "Patagon", who was to serve Shakespeare as a model for Caliban.

Patagonia is also a literary kingdom for Paul Theroux. Its mere physical existence, conveniently remote, refuels the fantasies it inspires, making the search for "emptiness, desolation, the suspension of intellect" less improbable. It's the place one would go to, like W. H. Hudson, to listen to the silence, and to ask oneself ("lawless and uncertain thought") what might happen if one were to shout out aloud.

Probably neither Chatwin or Theroux would find these photographs of Bariloche particularly interesting. Theroux wrote his "The Old Patagonian Express" without ever penetrating Patagonia. His journey finished at the gates of 'nowhere'. And Chatwin shows little patience with the people who briefly passed through his life on his journey through what was for him a fatally attractive land. Nevertheless, this hypothetical disinterest in everyday life does not invalidate the fantastic world that they perceive, nor does it diminish the

[20] Bruce Chatwin and Paul Theroux, *op. cit.*

reality of the other Patagonia, so visibly seductive.

These photographs establish a series of connections between the two realities. The chronology and historical information form the basic framework. The background is in counterpoint; how is one world invented and named by another; how does fiction precede reality; how do ideas determine what one sees; how are strangeness and fantasy sometimes transformed into literature, and how does literature sometimes transform fantasy into a moral concern?

Here there is no nightmare of an everwatching mirror; just fragments of the past.

II

"All aristocratic life in the later Middle Ages is a wholesale attempt to act the vision of a dream."
J. Huizinga[1]

*R*ETURNING to the matter in hand, let us look at two episodes which occurred near Bariloche in the seventeenth century.

According to available documentation, the first Spaniard to arrive at lake Nahuel Huapi was Captain Juan Fernández, who in 1620 had left from Calbuco, opposite the island of Chiloé, with forty-six

[1] J. Huizinga. *The Waning of the Middle Ages.* Penguin Books, 1979.

men. His purpose was twofold: to capture natives and to discover the "Ciudad de los Césares".

Credit for the main motivation for this Andean crossing, as a result of which the name "Navalhuapi" was to appear in a Spanish chronicle for the first time[2], may fairly be given to the attractive fiction of this legendary lost city, rumoured to be somewhere in Patagonia and sought in vain by so many expeditions. Amongst these, as we shall see, was that of Juan Fernández.

The legend is in turn based on the agonizing collapse of a real city, "Rey Don Felipe", founded in 1584 by Pedro Sarmiento de Gamboa on the north coast of the Magellan Straits, a few kilometers to the west of present-day Punta Arenas[3]. Survivors

[2] Juan M. Biedma. *Crónica histórica del lago Nahuel Huapi.* Emecé Editores, Buenos Aires, 1987.

[3] Several historical episodes have been instrumental in the creation of this legend. One of these is the part played by Sarmiento de Gamboa. A port was established on the Magellan straits for the purpose of controlling maritime incursions (such as that of Drake) at the extreme tip of the Spanish colonies. This was not an unfounded precaution. According to information supplied by John Maynard Keynes (*A Treatise on Money*, London, 1930), booty brought back by Drake on the *Golden Hind* paid a dividend of 4,700%, and "may fairly be considered the fountain and origin of British Foreign Investment. Elizabeth paid off out of the proceeds the whole of her foreign debt, and invested a part of the balance (about £ 42,000) in the Levant Company. Largely out of the profits of the Levant Company there was formed the East India Company, the profits of which, during the seventeenth and eighteenth centuries, were the main foundation of England's foreign connections".

of this failed settlement, who were last seen making tracks, perhaps fleeing, into the vast Patagonian interior[4], reappear in folklore some years later as a wealthy race, fair haired and thickly bearded, blue eyes gazing from under the brim of their three-cornered hats. These resurrected wretches had become the citizens of the "Ciudad de los Césares".

The city has been repeatedly described. Pedro de Angelis, compiler of various tales of journeys in search of it, tells us: "In order to have an idea of their richness it is enough to know that in their houses the inhabitants sat on golden benches… They spoke a language unintelligible not only to the Spanish but even to the Indians"[5].

Francisco Cavada[6] relates that "… it is ordained that no traveller shall discover it (the city) even when he is standing on top of it… The church tower is crowned by a great golden cross. If its bell were to strike, the tolling would be heard the whole world over."

Julio Vicuña Cifuente places it in the Andean Cordillera, on the shores of a great lake, and notes that "the same people who live there built it… for in the 'Ciudad de los Césares' no one is born and no one dies. The day the

[4] According to the tale of one of the survivors, Tomé Hernández, picked up by Thomas Cavendish on his 1587 expedition.

[5] Pedro de Angelis. *Colección de obras y documentos relativos a la historia del Río de la Plata.* Buenos Aires, 1910.

[6] Francisco Cavada. *Chiloé y los chilotes.*

city's spell is broken will herald the end of the world; for this reason nobody should try to discover its secret".

Silvestre Antonio de Roxas, held captive for a time by Pehuenche Indians, claims to have been inside the "Ciudad de los Césares", and in his description goes as far as to name the trees growing there: "cedars, poplars, oaks, orange and palm trees". And, even though none of these is native to the region, he affirms that "Nobody should think I have exaggerated in what I say, for it is the absolute truth; I was there and touched everything with my own hands"[7].

Juan Fernández was never to espy even from afar the golden cross of the church, far less the drawbridge which would lead him to the other side of the city wall, and to the streets which would take him to the heart of the mystery. But there can be no doubt that it was this dream which impelled him to travel, which led him to his encounters with strange, new people and lands, and which did open the way to one genuine place, "Navalhuapi".

(It might perhaps be fair to expect that, retold in some new version confused with the passing of time, his journey, extraordinary as most of the conquistadores' journeys were, would be remembered as successful, and that Juan Fernández and his forty-six

soldiers be said to have actually entered the "Ciudad de los Césares", thus crossing the frontier between fiction and reality.)

The second episode is a variation of the first –different actors, different names, but the same literary atmosphere pervades the historical events. In 1650 Captain Diego Ponce de León left Fort Boroa with sixteen Spanish soldiers and a thousand Indians. His intention too was to capture natives. He crossed the Andes and at Epulaufquen, which in English means "two lakes", found the Indians he had set out to capture –headed by two Dutchmen and a negro. All three were deserters; the negro from Alvarado's fleet and the Dutchmen from Prince Brouwer's. (Brouwer was a pirate who in 1643 "looted, destroyed and burned" the city of Castro on the island of Chiloé[8].)

There was a battle, which began on the water. The Indians resisted, and the Spaniards, aboard log rafts, were harried from "fast and easily maneuverable"[9] canoes. Their "tenacious" resistance was not enough, however, to prevent a Spanish triumph. Few natives were able to escape, but their leaders, the three deserter seamen, managed to get away "across the pampa in the direction of Buenos Aires".

These episodes might have inspired a novel such as "The War at the End of the World", by Mario Vargas Llosa

(also based on real events which occurred in the north-east of Brazil) and seem to echo Conrad's "Nostromo". Certainly the two Dutchmen and the negro remind us of Lord Jim, of Marlow and of Kurtz, and would undoubtedly have appealed to the author of "Heart of Darkness".

Because of the confused nature of such encounters, episodes like this tend to contain elements of both the real and the imaginary, but there can be no doubt that they did in fact occur. And the chronicles in which they appear are the first pages in the history of Bariloche; linear and discontinuous histories, punctuated by omission, through which we obtain only fleeting glimpses of groups of armed Indians, inhabitants of regions soon to be abandoned, leaving behind no image or likeness beyond the shadow of their departure.

Behind the dreams, behind the failure to find lost cities and the head-on clash with the Indians, lies another contrast, less attractive, less superficial; a contrast between the world across the Atlantic which the Spaniards carried in their memories, and the world, unmentioned in the chronicles, of those who were now living in this new land opened up by the conquest.

It is dangerous to presume too much about these times; to talk in terms of "Spaniards" or "Europeans" in the sixteenth century, or even less of that vague entity peering out of the pages of the chronicles, the "Indians", all but voiceless beings brought to life only

[7] Silvestre Antonio de Roxas, in Pedro de Angelis, op. cit.

[8] Juan M. Biedma, op. cit.

[9] Ibid.

through the mention of their adversaries. These groups and the way in which they interacted evoke a wealth of connotations that defy the imagination, but of one thing there can be little doubt: the Spaniards and the Indians inhabited very different worlds.

The first settlers in the Nahuel Huapi region were Fathers of the Company of Jesus, founded by Ignatius Loyola in 1540. Biographies of Loyola show that Iñigo López de Recalde, before his conversion, lived the life of a courtier and a soldier. "His mind was filled with the military and amorous adventures of Amadis of Gaul and other fictional heroes"[10]. He hunted and involved himself in duels and romances. When in 1521 Pamplona was besieged by the French, "almost alone at a council of war, Iñigo López de Recalde advocated resistance to death in the fortress above the city"[11] and prepared himself for death, confessing to a comrade in arms. He received a knee wound from French artillery and, as the battle ended and the fort surrendered, he was attended by the enemy. During his convalescence, for want of the chivalric tales he preferred, he read a life of Christ and a book of lives of the Saints ("The Golden Legend", by Jacobus de Voragine). This was in some way to change his life, and from that moment on he decided to devote himself to the imitation of Christ and the glory of God. He went as a pilgrim to the Holy Land, and spent the night before leaving on his knees, in full armour, praying before the Virgin Mary, praying over his arms and then renouncing them. On the other side of the Mediterranean, in Manresa, after a period of fasting and meditation, he wrote his "Ejercicios Espirituales" ("Spiritual Exercises"), the aim of which is to free the soul from its bonds and raise it to the will of God. The observance of these exercises, which deal with memory, imagination and understanding and are based on his personal experience, requires some four weeks.

The Recalde motto is "Gentle in manner, strong in action", and that of the Society of Jesus "Ad Majorem Dei Gloriam". Jesuits left for evangelical missions in Africa, China, and the Americas, all for the greater glory of God. St. Ignatius, General of the recently founded[12] order, kept contact with the earliest missionaries, his letters reaching them at their remote outposts. These letters took months, sometimes years, to arrive, and more than seven thousand of them have been documented.

J. Huizinga in "The Waning of the Middle Ages" (a book suggested to him as he struggled to understand the images created by the Van Eyck brothers in their paintings) has striven to recapture the flavour of this historical period which produced figures like Saint Ignatius. It is a work of perseverance and erudition, unexpected reflections ("It would be interesting to study from the point of view of physiognomy the portraits of that time, which for the most part strike us by their sad expression") and meditations on the nature of everyday life ("The modern town hardly knows silence or darkness in their purity, nor the effect of the solitary light or a single distant cry"). To paraphrase Huizinga, in the late Middle Ages horrendous crimes were publicly punished by atrocious measures, knights wore their ladies' colours, and from their pulpits priests moved the faithful to tears ("tears were considered fine and honourable"). A prince lived surrounded by passion and adventure. Processions of barefoot pilgrims walked the streets and the chivalric orders represent, after religion, "the strongest of all the ethical conceptions which dominated the mind and the heart".

These were times in which man lived tortured by the fear of death and the brevity of all earthly glory, by visions of the everlasting fires of hell and eternal separation from God. Dennis the Carthusian, for example, asked his followers to imagine a mound of sand as large as the universe, from which every hundred thousand years one grain would be removed. After an immense time the mountain would disappear, but the sinner's torment would be in no way lessened.

The imagination provided a devastating power to inspire fear and

---

[10] John F. Broderick, S. J., in *The Encyclopaedia of Religion*, vol. VII, M. Eliade Editor in Chief. Macmillan Publishers, 1987.

[11] Ibid.

[12] The statutes of the Society of Jesus were confirmed canonically by Pope Paul III in 1540.

panic, comments Huizinga. Happiness and heavenly glory, on the other hand, are mute. Mystics allude to the ecstasy induced by total denial; denial of images, of established patterns, of dogmas, "all that is culture is obliterated and annulled". The power of symbols in the late Middle Ages and its weakening in the hands of the mystics is the central theme we are invited to reflect upon in Huizinga's book.

During this period, he tells us, reality is tranformed into a series of images which become fixed and have their own place in the order of things. He calls this the systematic idealism of the Middle Ages. The most immediate risk of this practice is that, once reality is organized into symbols, what is personal or pertains to the individual ceases to be of any importance. The mind does not perceive shades or exceptions; it looks for "models, examples, norms". In order to explain things it does not analyze them, "but looks up to heaven, where they shine as an idea".

This tendency to ignore complexity is upset by the contrast between the old world and the new, whose disorder, like that of the mystics, disturbs the balance.

This invisible conflict took place in the minds of the Jesuits who began to arrive in Nahuel Huapi in 1670. Their lives illustrate perfectly the way people act and feel in Huizinga's world. They can also be seen as an example of the insularity of such stereotyped people and of the lengths they were prepared

to go to in order to maintain their illusion and to impose it on reality.

Father Mascardi, founder of the Nahuel Huapi Mission, began by rejecting his aristocratic Roman family. Giving up wordly goods and status is one of the attributes of a saint. Then he chose to become a missionary in a remote region, the island of Chiloé, in the South of Chile. Here he conceived a twofold plan —to cross the Andes, where he could convert the Indians on the other side of the Cordillera, and to go in search of the lost "Ciudad de los Césares". From the headquarters of the mission, a chapel and a hut on the banks of lake Nahuel Huapi, he made four journeys inland, fascinated —just as Captain Juan Fernández before him— by the thought of the golden cross, the crowning glory of a Utopian city. His fourth journey was his last. In 1673, at an unknown spot presumed to be near Puerto Deseado, he was killed by natives, his head crushed by bolas and his breast pierced with arrows[13]. Father Mascardi knew he would die. In a letter written earlier he forgave the Indians. The circle, ending in martyrdom, was complete.

We might also consider the case of Father Laguna, who crossed the Andes "barefoot, carrying a cross and a bag in which were a breviary and his devotional books", and who died consoling those who wept for him. Or that of Father Diego de Rosales, who

[13] Juan M. Biedma, *op. cit.*

became a soldier and "caudillo" in defence of the fort of Boroa, in the south of Chile, cut off from all outside help by the native rebellion of 1655.

What happened to Father Guillelmo shows us another side of the fascinating Jesuit experiences on the shores of Nahuel Huapi: the inevitable compromise between the ideal and the real.

One of the main problems faced by the mission was its isolation[14]. Communication with the nearest cities, in Chile, meant a journey of several days along the "lake road" used by Juan Fernández in 1620. There had also been, however, a land route, the "Vuriloche" pass, shorter and more direct, used earlier by the first conquistadores of Chile, and Father Guillelmo, turned explorer, was able to rediscover it. This was a practical measure which put the mission on a sounder footing.

Father Guillelmo also comes closer to reality in his psychology. He learned the Mapuche language, put together a Tehuelche phrase book, and wrote a Puelche grammar. This was the first attempt to see things through the names given them by others; the first

[14] In 1689 the Governor of Chiloé recommended to the Jesuit leaders in Chile that the mission in Nahuel Huapi should be closed. In his work Biedma gives Enrich's explanation: "At that time the Spanish authorities believed they should be responsible for providing food, shelter and protection for their missionaries, and in the last resort for avenging any affront that might be caused to their religion or person". The difficulty of communications between Chile and Nahuel Huapi was a complication for such an eventuality.

step in the complicated process of translation[15].

During the years in which the Jesuits were attempting to convert the Tehuelche, Mapuche and Puelche Indians, native Americans were the centre of a fierce intellectual debate. Now that it had been accepted that the lands discovered by Columbus constituted a New World, people inevitably began to wonder about the origins of the men who populated them. The creation of heaven and earth, of all living creatures and the first man –these were explained in the Holy Scriptures, but neither the New World nor its strange inhabitants were foreseen in sacred texts or those of classical antiquity, the secondary authoritative source. Until the beginning of the 18th century the theories and hypotheses put forward to explain the origin of America's indigenous people were little more than a complicated attempt to acommodate them within the schemata of the known and the familiar.

Paracelsus postulated, for example, that God created a second Adam for America[16], and Isaac de la Peyrère supports this idea in two books, "Prae-Adamitae" (1655), and "Systema Theologicum ex Praeadamitarum Hypothesi. Pars Prima" (1655). Based on the biblical passage which puts the existence of sin before that of Adam (Romans V 12-14), and on the stories of a dual creation (Genesis I and II), he suggests that God first created the Gentiles (who subsequently dispersed throughout the world, including the Americas), and then Adam, the founder of the tribes of Israel which play such a prominent part in biblical tales.

According to la Peyrère, only the Hebrews were destroyed by the flood, the Gentiles being spared, their existence attestable today in the ancient cultures of Egypt, Mesopotamia and the Americas, each of which had evolved in isolation. In the same year that la Peyrère published his books at least twelve other works appeared to refute his theories.

An additional problem was the fact that animal species in the New World were different from those of Europe. Sir Thomas Browne, in his "Religio Medici" (1640) wondered why America did not contain "that necessary creature, a horse" and how it was possible that all animals "including those not found in this triple continent" (Asia, Africa and Europe) could have come from one and the same place: Mount Ararat. "In Scripture" –reasoned Browne– "there are stories which surpass the tales of poets."

The Spaniard Juan de Torquemada wondered if the animals might have been transported by angels[17]. Gregorio García, on the other hand, had no difficulty in seeing them merely as monsters, degenerate forms of known animals[18].

Space does not permit a deeper study here of the uncertainties and reflections caused by the discovery of unknown animals and "true men"[19] in the New World. Some, like Diego Andrés de Rocha[20], thought the men of America were the descendants of Basques who, after the flood, had crossed the Atlantic to America. The ancient Iberians, adduces Rocha, just like the Indians, "ate and slept under the stars", and, just like them, had no time for science and no knowledge of money.

Amado de Villanueva somewhat radically affirmed that it was possible for man to be created by means of alchemy. It was otherwise suggested that the native Americans were Carthaginians, or Phoenicians; that they were descendents of the Welsh Prince Madoc, or of the ten lost tribes of Israel. Some believed that the

[15] Father Guillelmo's grammar and phrase book are lost, burned in a fire which destroyed the mission in 1713. He himself died in 1716, thought to have been poisoned by the Indians.

[16] Lee Eldridge Huddleston. *Origins of the American Indians, European Concepts, 1492-1729.* University of Texas Press, 1972.

[17] Juan de Torquemada. *Primera (segunda, tercera) parte de los veinte i un libros rituales i monarchia indiana, con el origen y guerra de los indios occidentales.* Madrid, 1613.

[18] Gregorio García. *Origen de los indios del Nuevo Mundo e Indias occidentales.* Madrid, 1607.

[19] The expression appears in the Papal Bull *Sublimus Deus* issued by Paul III in 1537. Textually it reads "...the natives are true men and not only capable of understanding the Roman Catholic faith but desirous of receiving it".

[20] Diego Andrés de Rocha. *Tratado único y singular del origen de los indios del Perú, México, Santa Fe y Chile.* Madrid, 1681.

Indians of the Yucatán peninsula were descendents of the Greek Ulysses, or that the inhabitants of Chile came from the Frisian islands, because "Chile means cold", and that is the prevailing climatic condition of the islands close to Greenland.

The total readiness to believe such suggestions, freely inspired by linguistic comparison or a liberal interpretation of ancient classical texts, must be understood as part of the attempt to "give these foreign lands our own form"[21], to come to terms with a discovery the complexity of which was summarized in 1537 by the Portuguese Pablo Núñez: "New islands, new lands, new seas, new peoples, and, what is more, a new sky and new stars".

Lee Eldridge Huddleston, in his analysis of European literature up to the seventeenth century concerning the problems of the origin of American man, concedes that the arguments are sometimes ridiculous but "in general, serious"[22]. Investigative methodology has changed in our day. Standard texts are produced by anthropologists rather than theologians, to "train the new generations". Huddleston sees however a similarity in the way they approached the subject. Yesterday's theologians, like today's anthropologists, were professionals who applied their methods with the greatest efficiency possible.

And certainly the Jesuit Father José de Acosta, one of the authors examined by Huddleston, is strikingly modern. He spent sixteen years (1570-1586) as a missionary in Perú. In his "Historia Natural y Moral de las Indias" he relied on direct experience rather than classical texts to come to terms with the New World. He paid little attention to hasty comparisons and tenuous associations between the European and American peoples, and had no time for theories not based on what we might call "common sense". He reasoned, for example, that if we accept that the natives have Jewish origins then we must also accept that they have forgotten "their lineage, their laws, their ceremonies, their Messiah, and finally their Judaism"[23]. He preferred to believe that the "New World which we call the Indies" was not completely separated from the "other world", and that there must be a land passage, to the north or the south, through which several waves of men and other classes of animals must have made their way. Acosta also recognized the dignity of these people and their institutions; he does not treat them as "mindless" people. In the middle of the sixteenth century, drawing on his own personal experience and shunning misguided appeals to classical authority, Father Acosta foresaw the discovery of the Bering strait, conceived the idea of ice ages which unite or isolate continents, and even anticipated the

principles of anthropology: to acknowledge the value of another person's being and actions, whether he be called "native", "aborigine", . "Indian" or whatever.

We can only conjecture how much of this background of doubt and vacillation the Indians could note in the Spaniards with whom they came into contact. The chronicles mostly tell us of battles, captures, and surrenders, group activities which give little hint of what was happening in the minds of the protagonists. Original testimony does give us some idea of what they were thinking. For example, a letter of some one thousand two hundred pages, with four hundred drawings, sent by the cholo Felipe Guaman Poma de Ayala to the King of Spain, was recently discovered in the Royal Library of Copenhagen. We might also mention the "Royal Commentaries" of the Inca Garcilaso. But works like this, when they exist at all, are very rare in conquest literature.

Texts left by the Jesuits at least show that the ethnographic map of the Nahuel Huapi region was considerably more complex than it would be in the nineteenth century, that era of independence and desert conquest which was to add a new dimension, that of the region's own ethnic history, to the other history brought by the Spanish conquerors.

Who were the "rebel Indians" said by Father Rosales to have lived on the islands in Nahuel Huapi? Or the Puelches, "people from the East",

[21] Hernán Pérez de Oliva. *Historia de la invención de las Indias.*

[22] Lee Eldridge Huddleston, *op. cit.*

[23] Joseph de Acosta. *Historia natural y moral de las Indias, 1590.*

whose language differed from Mapuche? Or the "anthropophagi" who inhabited the lands to the south of mount Tronador? These and other groups further away from the "cordillera" began to disappear with the conquest, or to fade away under the political hegemony imposed by the Araucanos (Mapuches) in a good part of Patagonia and the Pampas[24].

Faced with this long list of conflicts and the obvious differences in values which caused a barrier to be created between the two worlds, we are unavoidably left with the impression that the central clash was one of psychologies; of the sensitivities of, in turn, the religious man, the conqueror, the settler and the Indian. Consider the Mapuches as they saw for the first time one man, Father Mascardi, coming down from the mountains with his cross. The Mapuches, when they die, become sun eagles, but continue to visit the living through their dreams. Their numerous gods married and had children, like German or Greek gods. They built morality on this and other beliefs "which is not savage or mindless, but worthy of respect". One can but dimly imagine the reactions and tensions generated by Mascardi's attempts at conversion.

[24] Reconstruction of the relationships between indigenous tribes in existence at the time of the first contact with Europeans and the story of their gradual "Araucanisation" continue to be among the most important problems pending in American anthropology, according to Dr. Alberto Rex González (*Una armadura de cuero patagónica*, in *Etnia*, 12, 1970).

Li Zhi, "one of the most original thinkers of all times"[25], reflected on Father Ricci, a Jesuit missionary, that: "Ricci has read all our classics. He speaks our language to perfection, writes our characters and knows how to conform to our social usages. He is a truly remarkable man"[26].

Li Zhi could not understand that a man of such intelligence could seriously contemplate converting the people of China.

III

"Out there in the heart of the country you seem to stand alone, with nothing nearer or more palpable than the wind, the fierce mirages and the limitless distances."
H. Hesketh Prichard[1]

*I*N the opinion of Simón Bolívar America was not discovered by sailors and conquistadores but by Baron Alexander von Humboldt. Certainly the latter's curiosity and enthusiasm mark him apart from such vigorous figures as Cortés, Pizarro or Sarmiento de Gamboa. Humboldt took adventure and the concern for science with him to the New World.

Humboldt wanted to describe the whole universe in one book. But not in a dry, mechanical way —his "natural

[25] Simon Leys. *The Burning Forest. Essays on Chinese Culture and Politics.* Henry Holt & Co., New York, 1986.

[26] Simon Leys, *op. cit.*

[1] H. Hesketh Prichard. *Through the Heart of Patagonia*, London, 1911.

history" ought to "stimulate and provoke feelings". To Humboldt, painting, poetry and the observer's emotions were formed of the same material as physical things.

Darwin considered his books a "rare union of the poetic and the scientific". Schiller, on the other hand, a contemporary and countryman of Humboldt's, criticized him in harsh terms: "His mind is that cold, dissecting kind that wants all nature to be shamelessly exposed to scrutiny; and with unbelievable impertinence he uses his scientific formulae, which are often nothing but empty words and narrow concepts, as a universal standard"[2].

For Schiller, the accumulation of observational data on insects, rocks or climatic conditions had no value. The mere suggestion that the countryside could be broken down into its components was abhorrent to him. Nature was something to be approached afresh each time, reverently, allowing one's senses to be invaded by the feelings the contact provoked. This is what distinguishes objective from subjective thinking, what Kierkegaard saw as the fact that while with the former everything moves towards a result, with the latter the result is omitted, because what is important is the individual and unrepeatable experience itself; "...an existing individual is constantly in process of coming to be", writes Kierkegaard; "which holds true of any

[2] Douglas Botting. *Humboldt and the Cosmos.* Michael Joseph, London, 1973.

human being who has not permitted himself to be deceived into becoming objective, inhumanly identifying itself with speculative philosophy in the abstract"[3].

Humboldt was not in agreement with those who had little respect for facts and clinical observation: "In every branch of physical knowledge there is nothing stable and certain but facts. Theories are as variable as the opinions that gave them birth. They are the meteors of the intellectual world, rarely productive of good, and more often hurtful to the intellectual progress of mankind". Unlike the conquistadores who preceded him he attempted to describe what he saw in his explorations of the Amazon and Orinoco. It was Francis Bacon who drew attention to the paradox that those who travel on the ocean, "where there is nothing to be seen but sky and sea", write diaries, not those who travel by land "wherein so much is to be observed". "Let diaries, therefore, be brought into use" is his advice[4].

In Humboldt we have, at last, someone to climb the mountains and sail the rivers of America, fired by the enthusiasm to study and record whatever he saw. Humboldt's "conquest" is of different kind: it only exists in the imagination, and is a conquest of symbols and the abstract over the apparent neutrality of perceptions. It is also an attempt to reduce the subjective and unrepeatable.

The final aim of physical geography was, for him, that of recognizing connections between the enormous diversity of natural phenomena. In his view these connections can be equally validly represented by science or art. He would surely have agreed with John Constable in defining painting as an experimental science, or with Leonardo Da Vinci, who considered the eye to be a window into the soul, "the primary means through which the brain can get access to contemplating, in a wonderful way, the infinite works of nature".

When in 1789 Humboldt obtained permission from the Spanish crown to explore the colonies in South America, he took with him experimental equipment such as a cianometer, to measure different shades of blue in the sky, and a Dolland balance, to measure the specific gravity of sea water. He also took the trappings of his eclectic endeavours (mineralogy, physics, chemistry and botany), his secret fascination for travellers' books and the ubiquitous curiosity and enthusiasm which gave his scientific enterprise its special romantic aura.

Humboldt spent four years exploring South America in the company of the French botanist Aimé Bonpland. One of his first observations, at lake Valencia, near Caracas, was on the effects of indiscriminate deforestation on the topsoil. The trees, he commented, "protect the earth from the direct action of the sun. They also protect the lesser vegetation which forms the forest floor, without which rain water would run, free of obstacles to stem its flow, washing the soil away and causing sudden floods which devastate the country". Either through ignorance or unmeasured exploitation, this happens all over South America today, even in Argentina.

Outstanding moments of Humboldt and Bonpland's journey were the 1,725 mile expedition up the River Orinoco, and the first attempt to scale mount Chimborazo, in Ecuador. (They reached the height of 19,266 feet, a record for those times).

After crossing the Andes, Humboldt measured the speed and temperature of the cold current off the coast of Perú, trapped in which, as in a bubble, the Antarctic plankton, penguins, cetaceans and other animals which depend on it are swept along towards the Tropics.

Tales of these somewhat magical explorations through jungles and across mountain ranges stimulated a number of naturalists to undertake the then daunting journey to the New World, observing and recording in Humboldt's style the country they crossed and all its resources. Two cases in point are those of Darwin and Wallace, who saw, in the adaptation of animals and plants to different climates and topography, material for a theory which would explain, in a manner perhaps generally more acceptable nowadays, the problem of the origin of the species. (Darwin himself admitted that he preferred Humboldt's account of his journey

[3] Soren Kierkegaard. Concluding Unscientific Proscript. Translated by David Swenson and Walter Lowrie. Princeton University Press.

[4] Francis Bacon. Essays. Everyman's Library, London, 1925.

through the Amazon rain forest to his own.)

Artists were reading Humboldt too. His idea that American landscapes, plants and animals should be scrupulously and meticulously depicted influenced the style of many painters who followed him up the Orinoco, the Amazon or across the Andes. It was no longer enough to paint a plant; one had to paint it in such a way that it was clear what species it was. This concept can be clearly seen in the water-colors Humboldt himself made of mount Chimborazo. In a landscape which recalls the detail and atmosphere of the paintings of Cándido López, Humboldt places llamas and cactus easily identifiable as such; different types of clouds at different heights; the tree line clearly visible on the slopes of the mountains. He also drew on the rock wall the names of the species which grew in each climactic zone. This was indeed a very complete attempt at representationalism.

Among the painters who were inspired by Humboldt, probably the two most important were Frederic Church and George Catlin, both North Americans, both explorers, both artists. Church, "the most spiritual of Humboldt's children"[5], specialized in landscapes. He visited South America twice, in 1853 and 1857, painting mounts Chimborazo and Cotopaxi, and the splendour of the Amazon. Catlin was, on the other hand, primarily a painter of indigenous peoples. In the 1830s he made several journeys to the American West. He was concerned with going to the rescue of "indigenous natural beauty which could now be depicted and appreciated for its own intrinsic worth", a beauty which he saw fated to vanish forever. His pictures were later to revivify the faces, garments, and activities of the original settlers of America.

Catlin's fame rests on the more than four hundred portraits and landscapes he produced in those years, and on his "Letters and notes on the manners, customs and conditions of the North American Indians", published in London in two volumes in 1844. The three journeys he made to South America in the 1850s, after meeting Humboldt in Europe, are less well known. His first two journeys took him up the Orinoco and Amazon rivers, over the Andes and into Perú, following the pattern set by Humboldt. The third, in 1857, was to Buenos Aires, and from there to the coastal provinces (in lighters and canoes), on to the "Salinas Grandes" (on horseback) and finally to Patagonia (in a steam ship of the Blue Star Line). All in all he spent nearly a year in Argentina, always painting the natives and travelling in the romantic style of his mentor. Some twenty oils survive from his travels round Argentina, most of them in the hands of the Smithsonian Institute and the Museum of Fine Arts at Richmond, Virginia.

The new style in American portraits started by Humboldt gave a better likeness of the original, as we can see today. Not only the "natural beauty of the continent" was "represented and appreciated in its real value"[6] but also its economic and political problems. In an essay he wrote on Mexico and Cuba, one of the first economic geographies devoted to a specific region, Humboldt proceeds to relate a country's resources and production to its population and political conditions. It is the kind or work which, for its well-informed content and humanitarian reasoning, must have awoken the admiration of Simón Bolívar.

Humboldt's influence reached Argentina through his travelling companion, Aimé Bonpland, hired by Pueyrredón to direct the Botanical Gardens, and through Hermann Burmeister, appointed by Bernardino Rivadavia as Director of the Museum of Natural Sciences. Also perhaps indirectly through Dr. Franz Fonck who in 1856, at the request of the Chilean government, set about the first scientific reconnaisance of Nahuel Huapi lake.

The North American historian William Goetzmann describes the end of the eighteenth and all of the nineteenth centuries as the "second age of discovery". The difference between this and the "first age" was the shift in perspective, caused by the way scientists and explorers represented the

[5] William Goetzmann. *New Lands. New Men.* Viking Books, New York, 1986.

[6] Katherine Manthorne. *The Quest for a Tropical Paradise; Palm Trees as Fact and Symbol in Latin American Landscape Imagery, 1850-1875.* In Art Journal, Winter 1984.

New World. No longer was it a question of finding a shorter route to the Indies –the conquest of trade routes was by then over–, it was a question now, as Braudel points out, of obtaining "new information about geography, the natural world, and the mores of different peoples"[7].

This is a period marked by the search for precision, in which there is no longer a place for such fantasies as mythical cities of gold and silver or Patagonian giants. Paradoxically, the climax of this search for precision (and of the second era of discovery) is the repeated finding of imprecision and relativism. In the intimacy of the material world the structure of the atom desintegrates in quantum mechanics; nobody replaces Adam, and the first day of creation of heaven and earth vanishes into infinite time and assumes the form of unpredictable physico-chemical encounters.

The United States, born in the middle of this second era of discovery, rapidly adapts, according to Goetzmann, to the "habits and rhythms" of which it is formed. "Americans", he tells us, "undertook their own investigation of remote islands and landmasses in the world, in the course of which they discovered a new continent, Antarctica, and they began the process of mapping the ocean floor... At no point was the United States exclusively preoccupied with the great interior frontier of North America"[8]. This affirmation is not only corroborated by Captain Wilkes' successful voyage around the world; inroads were also made into the Paraná and Bermejo rivers by Lieut. Thomas Jefferson Page, aboard the "Water Witch".

The panorama in Argentina was different. There are no signs of a clear policy of exploration of the interior. Nor did scientific missions set out from our country to explore the world. Only individual efforts are recorded, like those of Carlos and Florentino Ameghino, or of the Perito Moreno*. The Ameghino brothers revived with their imaginations the way the country and its fauna had been in lost geographical times. For George Gayland Simpson the Ameghino's team work should be regarded as one of the most remarkable and successful in the history of science.

The first person to arrive at Nahuel Huapi from the Atlantic was Moreno. His journey should perhaps be considered in the context of those made by other explorers in the nineteenth century. Livingstone, for example, lost in darkest Africa, in search of the source of the Nile; John Franklin, vainly seeking an Atlantic-Pacific passage between the Arctic islands and ice; or George Chaworth Musters, who in the company of a group of Tehuelches forged a way from Punta Arenas to Carmen de Patagones, in a sense completing Moreno's journey in reverse.

We should remember that this is the century in which solitary explorers immersed themselves in Siberia or the Australian deserts, and also the century in which anthropologists like Baldwin Spencer began another kind of exploration, that of the cultural world of wild, "primitive men", by going to live among them.

During this period of rediscovery, Patagonia attracted a good many scientist-explorers. Charles Darwin might perhaps head the list, but others, perhaps less well-known, like the Finn Vairo Auer, also passed through Bariloche. Auer, who wrote a doctorate thesis in his home country on lake formation, arrived in Bariloche in the mid 1920s, when roads had just been made into the Nahuel Huapi National Park. Auer studied the rock faces which had been exposed by road cutting to determine the botanical and geological history of the region. In subsequent journeys he expanded his research to the whole of Patagonia and Tierra del Fuego, and founded a tradition of comparative studies between the ecologies of Finland and Argentina which continues to this day.

One of the most curious books to come from an explorer of the Argentine South is H. Hesketh Prichard's "Through the Heart of Patagonia".

[7] William Goetzmann, op. cit.

[8] Ibid.

* The word perito, used extensively in the Spanish version of this text, means an "expert". Francisco Pascasio Moreno was appointed expert witness for the British Crown arbitration by which the border disputes with Chile were settled, and the word perito has since become an inseparable part of this famous Argentine's name.

H. Hesketh Prichard's expedition was financed by a newspaper, the "Daily Express", which immediately calls to mind Henry Morton Stanley, whose journey in search of the lost Dr. Livingstone was also at the expense of a newspaper, in this case the "New York Herald". But H. Prichard's journey was backwards into pre-history, in search of a specific animal, the Mylodon darwinii, *a species of giant sloth, known only from fossil bones and some remains of skin with fragments of hair still attached. It was above all this circumstance that encouraged the idea that it might be possible to attain a live specimen. In the authoritative opinion of Prof. E. Ray Lancaster, Director of the British Natural History Museum, it was possible ("I don't want to say more than that") that the animal "still exists in the mountainous regions of Patagonia"[9]. The English explorer failed to find his mylodon, but his book is a faithful document of what he saw on his journey, full of fascinating observations on everyday life in Patagonia at the turn of the century and magnificent descriptions of the countryside, all in a concise, restrained language. The expedition crossed the Patagonian pampa on horseback ("who, having once seen them, can forget the pampas?"). Facing the landscape, H. Prichard reflected: "A man accustomed to cities would here feel forlorn indeed... There is no possibility of being mentally propped up by one's fellow men". He greets Dr. Moreno, who "has to be*

[9] H. Hesketh Prichard, *op. cit.*

recognised as the great geographer of Patagonia", and describes pumas and guanacos, how he travelled with his group of horses, the character of the gaucho ("the basis of Patagonian life"), mirages resembling cavalry squadrons in movement, gullies which alternated with the pampa ("pampa and cañadón, cañadón *and pampa") as far as the eye could see, and further, and the incessant, overbearing wind.*

Although the text constantly shows, with some justice, the strong effect the landscape had on the spirit, at the same time it is a constant farewell to all redundant romantic notions. When he sailed on the "Primero de Mayo" from Buenos Aires to Puerto Madryn, H. Prichard was perhaps a privileged passenger in a group consisting mainly of immigrants.

The situation aboard the "Primero de Mayo" was more or less as follows: "There were not only a good many people, but peoples, on board; all habited in ragged ponchos with round fur caps or those pointed sombreros that one associates with pictures of elves in a wood. As wild looking a group were gathered for'ard as ever sailed Southward Ho! Germans, Danes, Poles, and heaven only knows what other races besides; each little party formed laagers of their possessions and resented intrusion with volleyfiring of oaths. There was one laager in which I found myself taking a particular interest; it was made up of two men, a woman, and her brood of children. Their only belongings seemed to consist of four

ponchos, a mate pot and a kettle, and a huge basket of cauliflowers. They crept in and entrenched themselves between the cauliflowers and the port bulwark in the waist of the ship. From there they did not move, but sat swaying their bodies during the entire voyage. Was Patagonia an "El Dorado" to which those people were journeying? On that dark night, as the ship slid groaning and creaking over the brown waters, the dark scene, lit by stray blurs of light, rather called up a memory of Leighton's picture 'The Sea shall give up its Dead'".

An uncomfortable, almost perverse idea accompanies one on a journey towards the "end of the world"; the idea that it will never end, never can end.

The Golden City is of course unattainable. And for that matter, despite the noblest efforts, neither is it ever possible to get to the bottom of anything because rules and references crumble.

IV

"Not once, nor twice, nor thrice, but day after day I returned to this solitude, going to it in the morning as if to attend a festival." W. H. Hudson. *Idle Days in Patagonia.*

"For the world is not to be narrowed till it will go into the understanding (which has been done hitherto) but the understanding is to be expanded and opened out till it can take in the image of the world." Francis Bacon. *The Parasceve.*

*T*HE word "photography", if translated from Greek, means to "draw with light". Light enters the lens of a camera from different angles, and the points of light are printed on the sensitive emulsions of a photographic film. In the dark room the photographer places his plates in a chemical bath, which concentrates emulsion salts in larger numbers over the lighter parts of the plate. In this way the photographer obtains a light and shade negative of what he first saw through his view finder. Light is again projected through the negative, and falling once again on to special paper slowly reassumes the shape of recognizable objects.

At first glance, this mechanical game with light seems appropriate, and the reality of the photograph undeniable. But the longer one looks at a photograph, the more the illusion of its exactness begins to vanish. "Who told you that the camera doesn't lie?" exclaimed Kafka. "Photography concentrates one's eye on the superficial. For that reason it obscures the hidden life which glimmers through the outlines of things like a play of light and shade. One can't catch that even with the sharpest lens. One has to grope for it by feeling... This automatic camera doesn't multiply men's eyes but only gives a fantastically simplified fly eye's view[1]." (Kafka's notion is perhaps a little extreme and incomplete: the automatic camera catches aspects of reality revealed on the plate that the photographer may never have seen —the plate is a stage where events continue to take place even when the viewer turns his eyes aside.)

The central theme of this brief introduction has been the shifting barrier separating the real from the fictitious. In few places is this frontier still so open and uncertainly defined as in Patagonia. We have used certain lasting images from Bariloche's history in our search for "the hidden life which occasionally shows through the external reality". Now we must return these images —Captain Juan Fernandez' mirages; the dreams of the Jesuit missionary Mascardi, killed under a hail of arrows in the vast, unknown desert; Pigafetta's half-naked, painted giants; and the last giant sloth, creature of the lost worlds which so amazed Ameghino— to the stream from which we have plucked them.

Bariloche is no longer as it appears in these pictures. "To govern is to populate", Alberdi's phrase, no longer rings through the limitless distance of a new country. The wooden houses, impeccably designed and built by Primo Capraro and the first immigrants, have been replaced by concrete structures, or have been lost in the continued growth of a greater, more cosmopolitan city. Welshmen no longer arrive in Patagonia to remake their country in a land that is green, empty and free. Files of Tehuelches no longer cross the plateaus and the gullies, searching for the sea in summer or the mountain forests in winter. At the end of the day, these images and memories are also tricks of light and shade, and will fade away into darkness.

We are left with the eternal giddiness which Darwin found in the deserted Patagonian plains, characterised more by what they lack than what they possess. Darwin, always looking for order and rational explanations, saw in these, "with deep but ill defined sensations", the last frontier of human knowledge.

It is in search of this heady frontier that Francis Bacon proposed to set off, armed with imagination "from the beaten and ordinary paths of nature, to generate and superinduce a New Nature or Natures"; to forge, from the visible New World, other new worlds of the intellect.

W. H. Hudson left his house on horseback every morning in search of the same frontier, and its measureless silence. "There I might have dropped down and died, and my flesh been devoured by birds, and my bones bleached white in sun and wind, and no person would have found them, and it would have been forgotten that one had ridden forth in the morning and had not returned."

Edgardo Krebs
Wolfson College, Oxford,
April 1989

[1] Gustav Janouch. *Conversations with Kafka*. In Susan Sontag, *On Photography*, Penguin Books, 1987.

Bariloche, my home

Neighbours pose for a picture during a forest outing, c. 1920. (Photo – Consuelo Garza de Cádiz collection.)

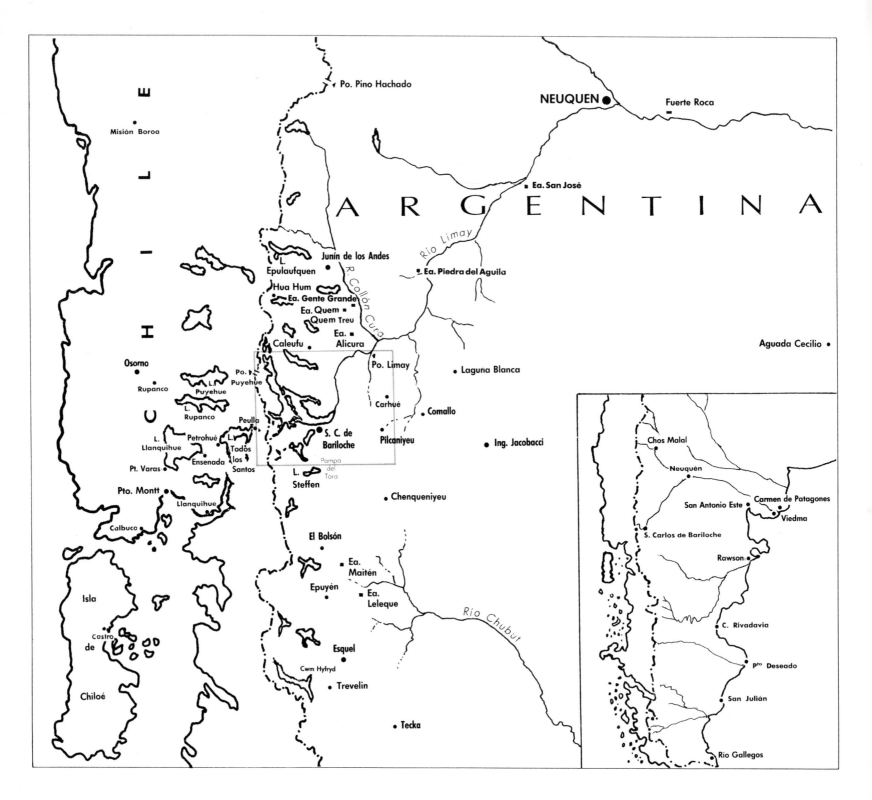

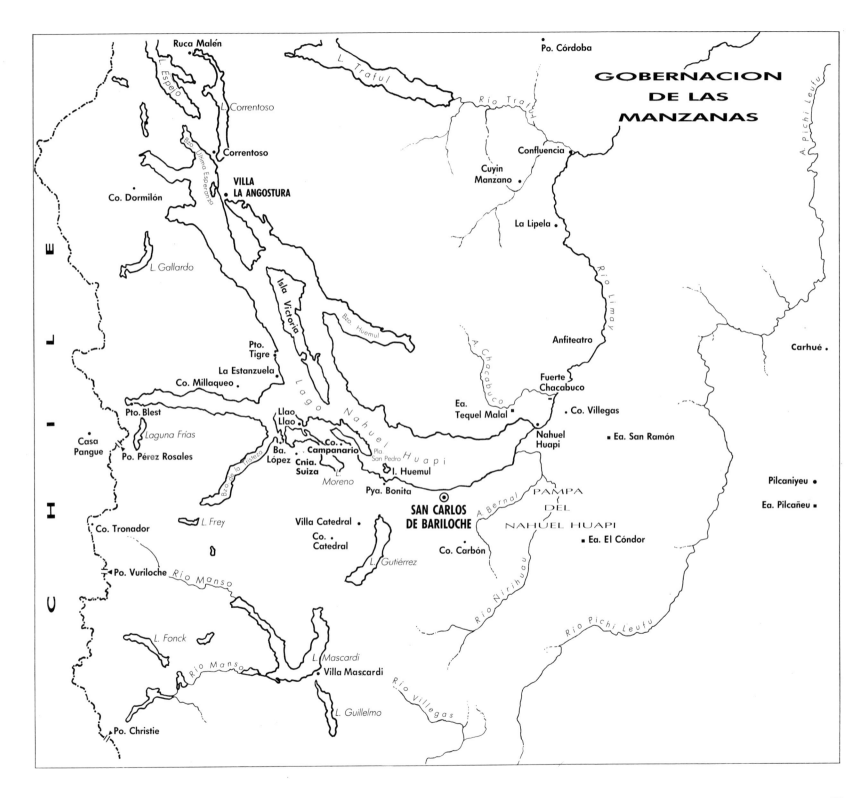

GOBERNACION
DE LAS
MANZANAS

Ruca Malén

L. Espejo

L. Traful

Po. Córdoba

Río Traful

A Pichi Leufu

L. Correntoso

Bzo. Última Esperanza

Correntoso

Confluencia

Cuyin
Manzano

VILLA
LA ANGOSTURA

Co. Dormilón

La Lipela

Río Limay

L. Gallardo

Isla Victoria

Bzo. Huemul

A. Chacabuco

Anfiteatro

Carhué .

Pto.
Tigre

La Estanzuela

Co. Millaqueo

Fuerte
Chacabuco

Co. Villegas

Pto. Blest

Lago Nahuel

Ea.
Tequel Malal

Ea. San Ramón

Laguna Frías

Llao
Llao

Co.
Campanario

Huapi

Nahuel
Huapi

Casa
Pangue

Po. Pérez Rosales

Bzo. de la Tristeza

Ba.
López

Cnia.
Suiza

Pla.
San Pedro

I. Huemul

Pilcaniyeu .

L.
Moreno

A. Bernal

Ea. Pilcañeu ■

Pya. Bonita

PAMPA
DEL

L. Frey

Villa Catedral

SAN CARLOS
DE BARILOCHE

NAHUEL HUAPI

Co. Tronador

Co.
Catedral

Co. Carbón

Ea. El Cóndor

Río Ñirihuau

Po. Vuriloche

Río Manso

L. Gutiérrez

L. Fonck

L. Mascardi

Río Manso

Villa Mascardi

Río Villegas

Río Pichi Leufu

L. Guillelmo

Po. Christie

THE Nahuel Huapi region has been inhabited since the earliest times by natives of the area. Around 1870 it formed part of the *Gobernación de las Manzanas*, or "Apple State", as the Indian chief Valentín Sayhueque styled his group of indigenous nations. These were times of war and conquest and Sayhueque, a wise and intelligent man, used every measure in his power to try to prevent outsiders invading his lands.

To this end he strove to mediate between different neighbouring Indian groups and to bring them together, while at the same time seeking peace and mutual respect with the Buenos Aires Government. However, the situation became untenable in 1879 when troops from the Andes campaign descended upon his territories and decimated or dispersed the Indian groups.

Valentín Sayhueque, chief and governor of the "Apple" People. (Photo – National Archives.)

Margarita Foyel

Traquel Sayhueque

Yemuil Llanquetru

Tanun Chagayo

Chief Chagayo

Halfbreed Araucano Indian

Sacac Inacayal

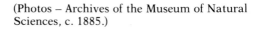

Araucano of the "Apple" region

(Photos – Archives of the Museum of Natural Sciences, c. 1885.)

PHOTOGRAPHS of "Apple" Indians, taken during their captivity in Tigre, Buenos Aires, possibly by the Samuel Boote photographic studio, at the suggestion of Francisco P. Moreno.

AS the military conquest of the "desert" was coming to an end the Buenos Aires Government began to consider legislation that would enable them to hand over these uninhabited lands in an orderly fashion. The most important legal instrument in this respect was the Ley del Hogar (Homestead Law), drawn up with the aim of offering plots of land to those prepared to accept the challenge of making a home in those regions.

Settling in the Bariloche area started at the end of the Nahuel Huapi campaign, on the 10th of April 1881, when the then Col. Conrado Excelso Villegas harangued the three brigades which, under his control, constituted the expeditionary forces, as they were assembled on the lower stretches of the river Limay .

"...the blue and white standard flies over lake Nahuel Huapi like a vanguard sentry of the nation ... many people will come to stand on the banks of this inland sea, and will find their reward by taking from the land the produce which providence allots to all who seek happiness in return for honest work."

Perhaps these words synthesize as well as any others the aim towards which so many strenuous efforts had been directed.

Chacabuco fort, as painted by Francisco Fortuny. (Photo – National Archives.)

Col. Conrado Excelso Villegas. (Photo – National Archives.)

IN 1883 a fort was erected, taking its name from the Chacabuco creek on the banks of which it stood, some one thousand metres from where the stream flows into the river Limay. No more than three huts made of mud and straw, a look-out post and a moat, it was built by soldiers under the command of Lt. Col. Nicolás Palacios, commander of the Third Brigade, who was never to see the work completed as he was, for military reasons, transferred further south.

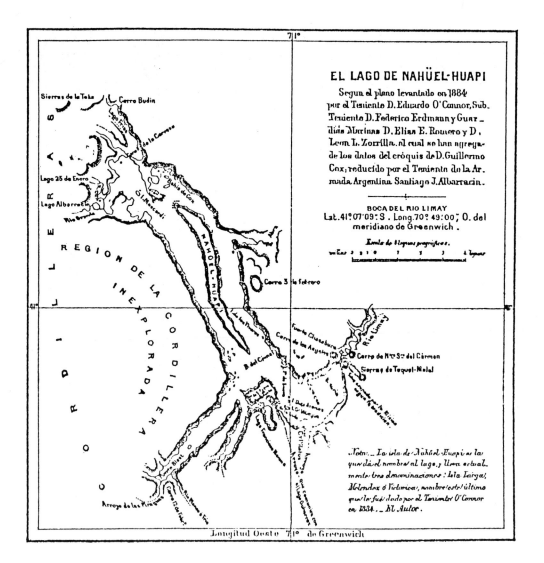

EL LAGO DE NAHÜEL-HUAPI

Segun el plano levantado en 1884 por el Teniente D. Eduardo O'Connor, Sub. Teniente D. Federico Erdmann y Guardia Marinas D. Elias E. Romero y D. Leon L. Zorrilla, al cual se han agregado los datos del croquis de D. Guillermo Cox; reducido por el Teniente de la Armada Argentina Santiago J.Albarracin.

BOCA DEL RIO LIMAY
Lat. 41° 07' 09" S . Long. 70° 49' 00" O. del meridiano de Greenwich .

(Photograph taken during O'Connor's expedition; archives of the Museum of Natural Sciences, La Plata.)

AS part of the Nahuel Huapi campaign a river expedition –under the command of Marine Lieut. Col. Martín Guerrico– left Carmen de Patagones on board the steamer *Río Negro*, charged with testing the navigability of the Limay river, reconnoitering the lake and establishing whether there might be a river passage through the mountains to the Pacific Ocean.

COMMANDER Pedro Diez Arenas was in charge of the fort at Chacabuco when the small river expedition passed through in 1883, on its way up the Limay under the command of Lieut. Eduardo O'Connor. The whaler in which the expedition was travelling had to be towed almost all the way past the confluence with the Collon Cura river; the *Río Negro* could not make further progress upstream and had had to turn back. On arrival at Nahuel Huapi they baptized the vessel with the name *Modesta Victoria*. This was the first time the lake had been sailed from end to end, and O'Connor, recalling the experience a year later, commented: "This region can rightly be called the garden of the Andes".

Camp on the island once named after General Villegas and now called Huemul, 1884. (Photograph taken during O'Connor's expedition; from the collection of the Patagonian Museum, Bariloche.)

Group of Mapuches photographed in Añihueraqui, near lake Quillén, to the north-west of Junín de los Andes, 1896 (Photo – Emilio Frey.)

O N the 8th December, 1882, Chief Curruhinca's tribe surrendered to the government. The previous year Chief Modesto Inacayal had, at the request of the army, abandoned the lands that he occupied next to the Limay river, and had moved further south to the region of Tecka, in the north west of Chubut.

33

WHEN the trooper Jarred Augustus Jones settled beside the now abandoned fort at Chacabuco in 1884, nobody else was living in the area. Jones was a genuine Texan cowboy who had become a Patagonian cattle rancher on occupying, under the homestead law, lands bordering the Limay, on the shores of Nahuel Huapi. Jones was still a bachelor, and he settled with the cattle he had received in payment from the Crockett and Newbery company, for whom he had just finished working as a cattle driver.

Many soldiers on the Nahuel Huapi campaign were discharged in the various places where the troops found themselves at the time, the intention being to populate these regions. The soldiers received their pay in the form of bonds exchangeable for land, but in order to redeem these it was necessary for the paperwork to be carried out in the capital, and in addition to contract land surveyors to fix the limits of the land, as the government measurements had only defined areas on a large scale and the land had not yet been subdivided.

Bureaucracy, journeys to the capital and surveyor's fees were beyond the means of these soldiers. The few veterans who remained in the area founded small and scattered rural settlements, frequently moving from one place to another in search of better water-holes or more adequate shelter from the wind and snow. They went from poverty to misery,

Jarred Augustus Jones, first rancher in the region and owner of the *Tequel Malal* estancia. The words mean "wooden corral" in the Mapuche or Araucano language. (Photo – Jones family collection.)

and their names are now forgotten; they lived far to the east of Nahuel Huapi and were soon to disappear completely.

Jones installed himself with some 1,500 head of cattle, an unusual number in those days. In 1893 José (Joseph) Tauschek and his family, a wife and two children, settled beside the lake. Tauschek devoted great care and attention to his fruit and vegetable gardens and his few head of cattle in a spot close to where today the railway crosses Route 237.

IN February 1895, a young man, thin and well dressed, stepped out of a small boat that he had run ashore on the beach of Nahuel Huapi, the sole occupant. Once on land his blue eyes surveyed the landscape: a stream, a small group of coihues (*Nothofagus dombeyi*, a southern beech), undulating prairies that stretched into the mountainous background...

He chose a spot where the mountain forests ended and the prairies began, and here the built his house, an advance guard for his future business. The name of this 29 year old was Carlos (Karl) Wiederhold, and it was his fortune to be the first white man to settle in what is today the urban centre of the city of Bariloche.

The place was some one hundred metres to the mouth of a nameless stream which today runs through pipes a few metres from where the civic centre stands. As time went by he devoted himself to gathering and selling wool, which he transported across the Andes through the Pérez Rosales pass. On his return journey he brought merchandise to sell to the isolated settlers.

Descendant of Germans, this pioneer called his store *La Alemana*, and it soon became a meeting place and business centre. Tradition has it that one day a settler in the Limay region, a Scot by the name of Enrique (Henry) Neil, sent a letter to Wiederhold but through poor knowledge of the language or perhaps by mistake, instead of addressing him as Señor Carlos, or Don Carlos, wrote San Carlos*. Wiederhold was much amused by this and grinningly showed the envelope to every customer who entered his store. He also changed the name of his business however –to *San Carlos*.

Hence the name of the city, the words "de Bariloche" being later added to distinguish the town from other towns with the name of San Carlos and alluding –through orthographic misrepresentation– to the Andean pass of Vuriloche, or Buriloche, immediately to the South of mount Tronador, in which direction a road led from the new settlement. San Carlos de Bariloche was from the start a name formed from two mistakes.

Carlos Wiederhold (1867-1935). (Photograph taken in 1925 by Enrique Lührs.)

* In English this would be "Saint Charles".

...*IN December 1894 I decided to travel from Osorno, through Puyehue, to Nahuel Huapi in order to experience those beautiful landscapes at first hand. I found few settlers in those times... I learned from Don José Tauschek that it was possible to make a passage between Nahuel Huapi and Todos los Santos... I then resolved to construct a road to carry fruit and merchandise and to open... a trading store... I built a cart road between Llanquihue and Todos los Santos... and between Peulla and Casa Pangue... and a trail to Puerto Blest. All this was done in one year, and between March and April I was able to carry a good quantity of merchandise. (Carlos Wiederhold.)*

(Photo of the San Carlos premises – Capraro family collection.)

WIEDERHOLD's small store soon grew into a prosperous business. In 1900 he brought the first commercial steamer to the lake, from Chile by way of the Pérez Rosales pass. The ship was transported in sections and reassembled in Puerto Blest, where it was named *Cóndor*. It weighed 60 tons, could carry 40 tons of cargo and could accommodate eight passengers.

The worthy *Cóndor* did sterling service, reducing the journey from San Carlos to the settlements in the South of Chile from seven days to only three. By comparison, the overland journey to Rawson or Viedma meant in those times forty to sixty days of slow travel by cart across the Patagonian desert. Here we have one of the reasons for Wiederhold's prosperity.

One of Don Carlos' plans was to make an agreement with the most important estancias of the region, enabling him to guarantee a constant supply of meat. Then he would open up a cannery which was to supply European markets.

He covered league after league on horseback, visiting farm managers. His neighbours claimed that Wiederhold and his entourage were recognizable from afar –they always trotted, as they did not know how to gallop. Trotting over such great distances was to affect his health, and he had to give up his ambitious projects and return to Chile, a sick man.

In its first year of operation the *Cóndor* carried 300,000 kilograms of merchandise, bound for the Pacific ports. (Photo – Frey family collection.)

Otto Mühlenpfordt, naval engineer, reassembled the ship in Puerto Blest in 1900. (Photo – Mühlenpfordt family collection.)

WHEN Francisco P. Moreno was appointed as the Argentine expert witness for the arbitration procedures with Chile, the Museum of La Plata formed an exploration commission. From left to right, standing: Ludovico von Platten (Danish), Carlos Zwilgmeyer (Norwegian), Gunnar Lange (leader, Norwegian), Juan Kastrupp (Danish), Juan Waag (Norwegian), Enrique Wolf (Norwegian) and Emilio Enrique Frey (Argentine); sitting: Eimar Soot (Swedish), Alfonso Schiörbeck (Norwegian), a person by name of Manterolo, not part of the committee, and Teodoro Arneberg (Norwegian).

There were only three Argentines among the officers of the commission; the *perito* Francisco Moreno, Roberto Guevara, engineer, and Emilio Frey, an auxiliary member. From observations made by Moreno and his colleagues the Museum of La Plata published, in 1897, *Preliminary notes on a journey through the territories of Neuquén, Río Negro, Chubut and Santa Cruz**.

(Photo – Frey family collection.)

The exploration committee began reconnaissance in the Andes region in January 1896. Here we see some of its members aboard an improvised raft on lake Traful. At the first pair of oars, Wolf and Schiörbeck; behind Juan Bernichan and Rodolfo Hauthal; with his back to us, Eimar Soot. (Photo – Archives of the Museum of Natural Sciences, La Plata.)

* In this work the Christian names of foreign participants, as was the custom, have been translated into Spanish and appear thus above. This policy has been followed throughout the present book.

THE various border commissions which worked on the frontier lands between 1897 and 1903 made many important geographical discoveries. They carefully studied the mountain chains and water courses, as Chile claimed a frontier on the basis of a continental division of waters, while Argentina sustained that the criterion should be a line linking the tallest peaks of the Andes.

The atmosphere was very tense, as it was not easy to find common ground for two highly-charged nationalistic countries, and finally Chile and Argentina agreed to turn to Great Britain as an arbitrator who could put an end to the controversy.

Border commission camp on the Tristeza inlet of Nahuel Huapi.

Placing provisional boundary stones. In the background is mount Tronador.

(Photos – Frey family collection.)

EMILIO Enrique Frey arrived in the region as an employee of the Border Commission. Here we see him at the age of twenty-four, seated on a white mule, next to an assistant.

Between 1910 and 1914 he was second in command of the Hydrological Studies Commission; then he was put in charge of the Bureau of Lands and Colonies, and from 1922 until his retirement he was Superintendent of the National Park of Nahuel Huapi. He founded the Bariloche Shooting Association in 1915 and the Bariloche Andean Club in 1931.

His enthusiasm, equanimity and love of the land in which he lived stamped themselves on the development of the region.

THE Border Commission established a base camp on the coast of the Nahuel Huapi lake, some 200 metres to the west of the present civic centre of Bariloche.

One day in 1902 news was brought by a group of tourists coming from the 16 de Octubre colony –in the area of Trevelin– that 44,000 kilometres of territory, out of the almost 96,000 square kilometres under dispute, had been recognized as Argentine. The news was celebrated with a lunch.

From right to left. Emilio Frey, Humberto Giovanelli, Aarón de Anchorena and Esteban Llavallol.

(Photo – Frey family collection.)

THE oldest road in the area ran from Fort Roca through Lake Blanca, Carhué, Chenqueniyeu and Maitén up to the 16 de Octubre colony, called Cwm Hyfryd –Pleasant Valley– by the spirited Welsh who planted wheat and raised cattle there. Another track joined Chos Malal and Carhué, via Junín. As far as transport and communication were concerned, the Nahuel Huapi region was as yet isolated from the outside world.

AT the beginning of the century settlers were scattered over a great part of Patagonia, mainly along the river banks, besides peat bogs –*mallines*– or close to the roads. As most of these people were illegally installed in the land they occupied, when surveying started an exodus commenced and many settlements were abandoned. It was generally some time until their homelands were once more peacefully occupied.

A covered wagon makes its slow way across a desert trail in Patagonia. (Photo – History Museum Collection, Neuquén.)

Cattle drive arriving in the area. (Photo – Frey family collection.)

Cattle station, 1904. (Photo - Carlos Foresti, Puerto Varas.)

THE Argentine Southern Land Company was set up in May 1889 to exploit 647,000 hectares of land suitable for cattle raising. The *Leleque* estancia was founded in 1892, followed by others by the names of *Maitén, Alicura* and *Pilcañeu.*

These estancias were well organised and extremely efficient. According to various contemporary witnesses, "if it hadn't been for the English who had come to the area, there would be nothing here now". This presumably refers to British capital investment as native ranchers of the time had little more to support them than their livestock.

Leleque estancia, property of the Argentine Southern Land Company. (Photo – A. de Anchorena.)

Celebration on the *Pilcañeu* estancia. (Photo – Manuel Cejas.)

A country anecdote tells of a certain native farm hand on the *Pilcañeu* estancia who, on account of his enormous stature, was called Juan Grande (Big John). He measured well over two metres and was renowned for his strength and his capacity for work. He was also alleged to consume a whole lamb, unassisted, for his midday meal.

The story goes that the farm manager, John Murray, had corralled off the finest breeding stock in all the area in a special enclosure, but every so often one of them would disappear without trace. There was no gate, and the fence was too high for any animal to leap out.

One day, while branding, John Murray shouted to Juan Grande amidst the tumult –"Juan, I bet you can't lift one of these onto your shoulders". "I'll show you if I can", replied Juan, and rising to the bait he hoisted an animal onto his back.

The mystery was solved. The missing cows were Juan Grande's dinner.

SEVERAL families had settled around the mouth of the Limay river, forming a small village near the *Tequel Malal* estancia. The head of one of these was Enrique Neil, who was in charge of floating wood-carrying rafts down the river; another Benito Boock, who set up as a blacksmith and cart manufacturer. Also living there were the Garay brothers, who ran a store and a freight business. In 1897, the year in which these territories came under national administration, José Luis Pefaure came to this spot, from that time onwards known as Nahuel Huapi; he was destined to be the first Justice of the Peace in the region.

Jones & Neil's store, 1902. (Photo – A. de Anchorena.)

AT that time this kind of judge carried three books around with him –one to record marriages, another for births and a third for deaths. It's interesting to see that in the year 1901 there were already 177 entries in the Births Register –one hundred and seventy seven children born in pioneer homesteads. And hopes for the future of these children were strengthened when, on May 3rd 1902, a Government decree was signed in Buenos Aires, allocating land on which to found their new town: *San Carlos de Bariloche*.

Enrique Neil, his wife and their son Diego Eduardo. The younger Neil worked for 45 years for the Argentine National Parks Service, and was Superintendent of the Los Alerces and Nahuel Huapi parks. (Photo – Mange family collection.)

San Carlos, March 1902. The flag shows that on that day news was received of the results of the British arbitration, through which it was established that the land on which the settlers were living was Argentine. (Photo – A. de Anchorena.)

San Carlos, inside the store. (Photo – Hagemann family collection.)

I N fact Bariloche was not founded by a single government decree, rather through a series of them. The most important is dated May 3rd 1902.

In compliance with the decree of 9th April inst. which in accordance with the Homestead Law authorises the foundation of a Colony denominated Nahuel Huapi on lands adjacent to the lake of that name, and in accordance with information received from the Bureau of Lands and Colonies,

THE PRESIDENT OF THE REPUBLIC DECREES:

Article 1. 400 hectares shall be reserved for the foundation of settlements in the following places: in the territory of Río Negro, in the place known as Puerto Moreno, lots 111 and 95; in the place denominated San Carlos, lots 114 and 115. In the territory of Neuquén: the isthmus situated between lots 9 and 10 and the lake shore bordering lots 1 and 4. An additional 5,000 hectares shall be reserved for the future agricultural needs of the colonies within lots 89 to 93, 95 and 111 to 115.

Article 2. The term fixed by article 5 of the aforesaid decree of 9th April inst. to receive applications for lots of these colonies in this capital shall be extended to 60 days. To be returned to the Bureau of Lands and Colonies and duly filed.

Signed: Julio A. Roca, President of the Republic; Wenceslao Escalante, Minister of Agriculture.

Perito Moreno Hotel, established in 1902.
(Photo – Hagemann family collection.)

The first school teacher, Zulema Jones, poses alongside her pupils. (Photo – González family collection.)

45

W HEN the government decree was sanctioned on May 3rd 1902, a few precarious houses were built in front of the *San Carlos* store. In the following month of June Captain Mariano Fosbery of the Fifth Cavalry Regiment, stationed in Nahuel Huapi, decided to set out a provisional street, so that, in his words, the town "shouldn't grow up crooked".

A group of soldiers began the work in front of the *San Carlos* store towards the east. One of the settlers volunteered to measure off the blocks, and in this way it was Don Benito Boock's fortune to indicate where the street corners should be.

This was the origin of the street now known as B. Mitre, and despite being plotted without the aid of a theodolite, the alignment turned out to be almost exact, as the engineer who came to carry out the official survey, Apolinario Lucero, was to discover when he began work on the 27th December 1902. Little by little, to the beat of no drum, the town began to grow...

The small house marked ① on the key corresponding to the photograph on the following page was the first school, in what is today Mitre 150. It had one classroom only, and was ruled over by Zulema Jones, an Argentine, daughter of Judge Justo Jones, an Englishman with jurisdiction over the Limay area, and no relation to Jarred Jones, mentioned earlier. The pupils were the children of Germans, Spaniards, Norwegians,

Nahuel Huapi Police Station, 1902. (Photo – A. de Anchorena.)

Italians, Arabs, Russians, French, North-Americans, Chileans and Argentines. The settlement of San Carlos de Bariloche was nothing if not cosmopolitan.

Where today the Banco Nación ② stands, Don Luis (Louis) Bonefoy opened up business as a butcher, and his meat, slaughtered there on the premises, sold at 10 centavos the kilo. Halfway down the street was the *Perito Moreno* Hotel ③, established in 1902 and attended by its owners, José Riveiro and his wife. They had rooms for twenty guests and a dining room where town events could be celebrated. When the *Cóndor* was approaching the port it would blow its whistle, once for each hungry guest aboard,

and in this way the whole town got to know if anyone new was arriving.

Number ④ corresponds to the home of the Alsina family; number ⑤ to a house built by the army, where police officer José Alaniz lived at that time; ⑥ was the telegraph office, opened in San Carlos on July 11th 1902; and ⑦ marks the "historic cypress", about which more anon.

1903. Corner of what today are B. Mitre and L. Quaglia streets, looking eastwards. The main buildings are indicated in the key on the previous page. (Photo – Capraro family collection.)

THE story of the tree known in local tradition as the "historic cypress" dates from Francisco P. Moreno's expedition to Lake Nahuel Huapi in 1880. One of the aims of this journey was to rediscover the legendary Vuriloche pass, an important strategic route for the natives of the region.

Once in the area, he realised that the chiefs Inacayal and Foyel resented his presence, this being made quite clear to him by Chief Valentín Sayhueque, Lord of the "Apple" people. Despite the warning Moreno made his base camp near Nahuel Huapi lake, in the shade of an enormous cypress*.

From this camp he made short excursions, returning one day to find a young Indian, awaiting him, who instructed Moreno that he was to "...come to our headquarters to receive further instructions..."

Thus on January 22nd 1880, Moreno's status changed from that of visitor to prisoner. He spent a peaceful night in captivity, for the Indians were not hostile to him, but the silence only seemed to underline the potential danger. During this tense rest, Moreno planned his escape. The following day, while being moved to Caleufu, he managed to slip his captors and make his way back to civilisation.

In 1896 Francisco P. Moreno once more arrived at lake Nahuel Huapi, this time as Argentine witness for

* *Austrocedrus chilensis.*

(Photo – Capraro family collection.)

the border arbitration with Chile. When he saw the cypress that had once offered him shelter and protection he wrote: "My journey that day was the most beautiful I have made in all my days as a traveller... cypresses and *alerces*** grew in profusion here... I measured one that day and its trunk, at the height of a man on horseback, measured more than eight metres in circumference. It was the tree that today stands looking over the town of San Carlos".

He baptised the tree *el venerable del lago*, which in English would be approximately "the grand old man of the lake" and it was remembered for years afterwards. It stood in front of the hospital until it was pulled down to widen the road in 1960.

** *Fitzroya cupressoides,* a relative of the giant sequoia of California.

IN another of his several journeys to the region, on April 12th 1902, after having successfully finished his work with the border negotiations, Francisco P. Moreno sailed on the Nahuel Huapi for the first time in the steamboat *Cóndor*, accompanied by Thomas Hungerford Holdich, the British arbitrator in the border dispute. Moreno became determined that this paradise of peace and beauty should never be spoiled, and the same day he sent a telegram to his friend President Julio A. Roca, in which he wrote: "I beseech you not to take any firm decisions on lands and forest in this area…".

In gratitude for his research, his expeditions and his skill in the border negotiations, the Argentine Government rewarded Moreno with three square leagues of land in the place of his choice. However, no sooner did he take possession of these lands, situated in the most beautiful part of the lakeland area, than he returned them to the Government, on the condition they be preserved in perpetuity as a national park for the enjoyment of present and future visitors.

Facsimile of letter in which Moreno donated to the Nation lands which he had received as recompense for his services in the border dispute. (Original in Patagonian Museum, Bariloche.)

TEXT OF MORENO'S LETTER
(Free translation)

Buenos Aires, 6ᵗʰ November, 1903

His Excellency Dr. Wenceslao Escalante,
Minister of Agriculture.

Sir:

I see from law Nº 4192 as published in the Official National Bulletin on 22ⁿᵈ August ult. that I am to be awarded, as recompense for my services freely offered to the nation before being named Argentine expert witness in the border dispute with Chile, state lands in the territory of Neuquén or the south of Río Negro.

In my travels through those regions at the time, for purposes which were to lead to my appointment, I much admired the exceptional beauty of the area and more than once spoke of how useful it would be for the State to set aside part of this land for the enjoyment of present and future generations, following the example of the United States and other countries which have superb national parks.

Today, through the above mentioned law, I find myself possessor of lands which, in far off days, gave me a glimpse of the future greatness of these then unknown territories, lands whose ownership was then under dispute but are now irrevocably Argentine, and I should urgently like to contribute to the realisation of ideals conceived while I was carrying out my work there, and which developed through my observations. For this reason I should like to request that an allotment of three square leagues be set aside in the region where the territories of Río Negro and Neuquén have their border, to the western end of the principal fjord of Nahuel Huapi, and that this should be conserved as a natural public park, and I hereby request Your Excellency to accept this, my donation to the country, once the limits of this land have been determined, of the area which extends from Lake Cántaro in the North to the Barros Arana gap in the south, having as its western limits the border with Chile through the Raulíes and Pérez Rosales passes and as its eastern limits the hills to the east of the inlet of Puerto Blest and Laguna Fría, this area containing the most interesting aspects of natural beauty that I have observed in Patagonia.

Each time I have visited this region I have told myself that, if made inalienable public property, it would soon become the centre of great social and intellectual activity; also an excellent barometer of human progress; as the physical and natural phenomena observed there begin to attract interested parties, who will give themselves over to their fruitful research and to the marvellous rapids and lakeside scenes, the great forests, the craggy peaks and the eternal snows and will find themselves in an unique geographical situation, halfway between Australia and New Zealand and the Atlantic washed shores of Europe. These phenomena constitute a special group of circumstances which favour my present proposal, in this beautiful sweep of Andean land, where with its summit Mount Tronador unites two nations in praise of whose natural union it will ever stand.

Chile possesses neighbouring public lands and it may perhaps be that in that tranquil place the inhabitants of both sides of the Andes can find the peace and rest, increasingly necessary

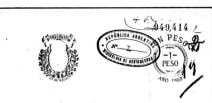

in today's tumultuous world, to solve problems that can not always be solved by diplomatic means. Visitors from all over the world, combining and interchanging their interests and feelings at this international crossroads, will benefit even more the natural progress of the influence afforded this part of southern America for its geographic conditions.

On making this donation I should like to state my wish that the present appearance of these lands should not be altered and that no more construction should take place than that which is necessary to cater for the visitors and such facilities as may be necessary to meet their requirements. Their presence in these parts will always be beneficial to these regions now bound together in natural sovereignty, and their planned presence here will soon contribute greatly to the future of the Argentine Nation.

I have the honour, Sir, to remain your most faithful servant,

Francisco P. Moreno

San Carlos, 1902.

Extension of the *San Carlos* store, property of the Chile-Argentine Society, 1904.

AT the end of the 19th century Don Carlos Wiederhold's store passed into the hands of a company, the *Sociedad Comercial y Ganadera Chile-Argentina* (the Chile-Argentine Cattle and Trading Society). The President of the company was Don Arturo (Arthur) Edwards, and the capital came from Germans who had settled in Chile, from the Edwards Bank in Santiago and from shareholders of the Chilean newspaper *El Mercurio*.

The growth of business activity was so sudden that by the year 1903 the company had about 300 employees. The management was mainly German while the workers all came from the island of Chiloé.

The few small tradesmen who were installed around Nahuel Huapi were severely affected by this, and approached the regional and national authorities to voice their worries.

Jetty, steamers and launches, San Carlos, 1904.

(Photos – Chile-Argentine Society.)

CONDITIONS in the Pérez Rosales Pass were improved by the company which bought Carlos Wiederhold's store, the Chile-Argentine Cattle and Trading Society. This, added to the lake journey, reduced the travel time from Bariloche to Chile from seven to three days.

Between Puerto Blest and lake Frías, in a boggy spot that even today can cause problems, they "paved" the road, that is they laid logs across the trail. In 1904 the company had 29 twin axled carts and 228 oxen, as well as horses and mules, working the pass; hotels in Puerto Blest, Casa Pangue, and Peulla, and 170 kilometres of telephone communications, in order to support this Trans-Andean service.

A journey from San Carlos to Puerto Varas in Chile implied the following: a trip on the steamer *Cóndor* from San Carlos to Puerto Blest, with occasional stops in López bay; then over the "paved" road as far as lake Frías; across lake Frías by boat; overland again until reaching overnight accommodation in Casa Pangue and Peulla. The following day by boat as far as Petrohué; then, by land to Ensenada, and finally across lake Todos los Santos in the steamer *Tronador* to Puerto Varas. From there it was easy to take the train to Santiago and then the Trans-Andean line through Mendoza to Buenos Aires.

Mules carry wool over the Trans-Andean pass, along the "paved" road, 1904.

The pass could be negotiated even in winter, 1902.

San Carlos, wool shipment. (Photo – Patagonian Museum.)

Chile-Argentine Society brochure, source of the two unattributed photographs on this page.

Main house, *San Ramón* estancia, 1904.

THE Chile-Argentine Cattle and Trading Society acquired the *San Ramón* estancia in 1901. In 1902 this was the first farm in the area to be fenced in. By 1904 the company owned the best lands in the region: the *San Ramón, San José, Piedra de Aguila, Gente Grande* and *Quem Quem Treu* estancias, among others, totalling some 322,000 hectares. They also owned an additional 30,000 hectares by Lake Nahuel Huapi, and leased another 162,000 from neighbours. They enjoyed a total of 514,000 hectares of the best land in what today are the provinces of Neuquén and Río Negro.

On the *Quem Quem Treu* estancia lived the Society's administrator, a German army colonel, Baron von Reichnacht, a bald, fat man, and somewhat forbidding in nature.

These cattle operations, in addition to the trading activity which extended from Nahuel Huapi as far as Comallo –90 kilometres to the east– and the transport lines through the Andes reaching the Atlantic coast at San Antonio –today called San Antonio Este– give a good idea of the size of this German-Chilean enterprise.

Trading store, Comallo. (Photo – Hagemann family collection.)

Stud farm. These jet black horses were bred from stallions brought from Buenos Aires, where they were used to pull hearses.

Cattle on *San Ramón* estancia. At that time long horns were bred for as much work was carried out by draught oxen.

(Photos Chile-Argentine Society, except left centre.)

WOOD cut from native forests was an important commodity in those days, both for local use and for dispatch to buyers far away.

Houses were built of Nahuel Huapi wood as far away as Viedma and Patagones, and a Canadian company transported logs in small rafts along the river Limay. Many of the principal houses on the earlier estancias were built with wood from the area, and cypress posts were used extensively for fencing in fields and boundaries.

Felling was controlled by the authorities, according to the criteria of the time, as can be seen from a telegram sent to Eugenio Tello, Governor of Río Negro, by Eduardo Beovide, Judge of San Carlos de Bariloche, in 1902: ...*The whole neighbourhood needs wood for the construction and repair of their houses, which can only be taken from the lake forests. If Your Excellency would like to authorise me, I could issue permits, under the strict control of the police, for wood to be cut exclusively for this purpose.*

This sawmill belonging to the Chile-Argentine Society stood in front of the present day Civic Centre, 1908. (Photo – Chile-Argentine Society.)

BARILOCHE port. In the foreground can be seen the jetty erected by Wiederhold in 1896 and, in the background, the one built by the Chile-Argentine Society in 1909.

Before the end of the century 300,000 kg of wool had left this port, and 93.000 kilograms of general cargo had entered, mostly provisions for the town. In a decree of the 23rd August 1904, the President of the Nation declared Bariloche a free port, a status it was only to enjoy for a brief period.

Postcard issued by the Chile-Argentine company.

The *chilote* Chivilcoy.

Chilotes, or natives of the island of Chiloé, in the south of Chile, provided a cheap if irregular work force, being employed as woodcutters or general labourers; they formed a large community which maintained its own culture and folklore. (Photo – Baratta family collection.)

GOOD quality wheat was grown in San Carlos de Bariloche, reaped with a scythe as the uneven ground did not permit mechanical harvesting. When presented in the Centenary Rural Exhibition in Buenos Aires, Bariloche's wheat won a gold medal.

However, like all wheat in the Cordillera, it had a very short life once harvested. This problem, compounded by the difficulties of transportation, limited its usefulness to local consumption.

Harvests were good however, and considerable areas of land were sown, mainly in the San Pedro peninsula, at lake Moreno, by Llao Llao, on the lower slopes of mount Otto, at the Estanzuela, at the foot of mount Millaqueo, and by lake Espejo.

The most important flour mill was at San Carlos, other smaller ones being found at San Pedro, Llao Llao and Estanzuela. This last mill belonged to the Eggers family, and was powered by a steam boiler.

Harvesting wheat on the San Pedro peninsula.
(Photo – Frey family collection.)

The corner of Mitre and Fernández Beschtedt streets, looking west, c. 1908. On the right can be seen Cornelio Hagemann's store, then Miguel Penna's home. Hagemann and Haneck arrived in the region with the Border Commission in 1898. (Photos above and on on left – Hagemann family collection.)

THIS waterwheel at the San Carlos flour mill was powered by the stream known in those days as *del Molino* (the Mill stream).

Originally constructed by Carlos Wiederhold, it was first used to drive a circular saw for cutting timber, and subsequently modified and, with the addition of a millstone, used to grind wheat into flour.

Hermann Haneck was the town miller. Working all year he produced some 3,000 kilograms of flour, when, which was not always, wheat was to be had. The photograph was taken in 1902.

View of the town, c. 1910; Moreno and Fernández Beschtedt streets. (Chile-Argentine Society postcard.)

Carts belonging to Enrique (Henri) Gingins, c. 1909. (Photo – Mange family collection.)

ONE day in 1902, on the banks of an inlet of Nahuel Huapi lake called *Ultima Esperanza* (in English "Last Hope"), two old friends, Federico Baratta and Primo Capraro, were reunited in the presence of Carlos (Karl) Junhans, an accountant with the Chile-Argentine Society.

Baratta had been living there for several years, and he invited Capraro to settle in the area. They both came from the same region of Italy, the Province of Belluno, in Veneto. Baratta was a mining engineer, and he and his friend tried their luck panning the nearby streams for gold.

Primo Capraro had left Italy to seek his fortune in America, stopping first in California, then in Arica, on the border of Chile and Perú, and finally in Nahuel Huapi. But luck passed him by, and he turned from gold to working with wood from the Bariloche forests.

Pioneers –Federico Baratta and Primo Capraro celebrating their reunion, 1902. (Photo – Baratta family collection.)

FEDERICO Baratta was the first person to request land in the newly established Nahuel Huapi agricultural colony. The national Government had agreed to create this settlement and authorised lots of 625 hectares on the edges of the lake.

Possession of these lands was granted through an engineer by the name of Humberto (Umberto) Giovanelli, a rotund, good-natured man who had arrived with the Border Commission and kept a small office in what is today Mitre 425.

Giovanelli was good at his job, trying to persuade everyone who came near him of the advantages of settling in the area. In many cases he was able to sway the minds of the undecided into parting with 500 pesos, the price of 20 cows at the time, in exchange for a plot in the new settlement.

Giovanelli found it easier to sell lots in the town, each lot being a quarter of a street block, which were assigned on the condition that they were to be built upon. This was a

deliberate attempt on the part of the Government to oblige newcomers to settle, but the results were meagre because of the enormous distances, the high cost of transport and the limited resources of the people who settled there. Nahuel Huapi was never to prosper in the way that had been envisaged.

A settler and his family at the Bernal creek. In the centre of the photograph, Angel (Angelo) Lavagnino, his wife and daughters; further back, Emilio Frey and Manuel Castro, 1903. (Photo – Frey family collection.)

Carrying wool. (Photo – Mange family collection.)

A cattle count carried out in the Department of Bariloche in 1902 by Judge Eduardo Beovide showed 28,500 cows, 95,000 sheep and 7,190 mares.

At the same time the Police Inspector of the territory, Mario Quiroga, reported that: *In the last year the number of settlers coming from Neuquén and other points has increased notably.*

Certain names appear as established ranchers before 1900: in Cuyín Manzano, a certain Asenjo; in Limay, José Dolores Alvarez, from Mendoza; in the Córdoba pass, a Mexican by the name of Córdoba, after whom the spot is named; Salustiano Vásquez was breeding cattle in Hua Hum as early as 1884; and Pedro Vásquez, alias Matoco (the name given to him when he was taken prisoner by Sayhueque in 1839), was the first to do so in Valle Nuevo, known today as El Bolsón.

The first breeders usually delivered their stock to Pacific ports.
The drive started along the Nahuel Huapi pampa, followed the course of the river Ñirihuau, crossed the river Villegas, reached the Toro pampa, where the Indian Nanchepay lived, skirted Lake Steffen and crossed into Chile through the Christie or Cochamó passes.

Each drove consisted of approximately 150 head of cattle, with six or seven hands riding herd. Occasionally wild or stray animals encountered along the way, would join up with the herd.

THE lack of bridges and, in some parts, even of tracks, made the journey from San Carlos to Viedma or Rawson extremely difficult, requiring some fifteen to twenty slow days travel across the Patagonian steppe.

Navigation on the Limay river was the usual form of transport for trade in those days, but this was extremely dangerous for passengers and their loads. Famous raftsmen of the time were the Macías brothers and a native of the region, Cheuquepán.

(Photos – A. de Anchorena, above, and Herbert Wechsler, centre.)

(Photo – Aarón de Anchorena, 1902.)

DRIVING a mule train was a real art. If only one animal balked it could cause a tangle of reins and trapping that could take hours to sort out.

The driver had to keep an eye on the ears of each animal during the trip. If the ears were erect and pointing forward then the animal was content and likely to obey commands; if they drooped forwards, the animal was tired; if one ear was lowered while the other stayed erect, something was bothering the mule; if the two ears pointed backwards then the mule was really upset, a sure sign of trouble.

Teams of oxen were also used but were much slower.

The arrival of a mule train was quite an event in the village. The names of certain muleteers are still remembered; Fermín Salaberry, for example, who later set up as a rancher in the vicinity of where the *Cóndor* estancia stands today; or Benito Crespo, who left mule trains for the Civil Registry Office; Salvador Gil; Santiago Sánchez; the North American Jeff Davis Wagner; or his colourful fellow countryman Martin Sheffield, famous for his tall tales.

Fleet of mule trains belonging to Ricardo Carro Crespo in Pilcaniyeu, 1915. (Photo – Manuel Cejas.)

Pablo Mange (wearing hat), a Spaniard who settled with his family on the Huemul inlet in 1906. Mange was primarily a fruit grower who wanted to start a cider factory, but he was also a good photographer, working as a journalist for the magazine *Caras y Caretas*. He founded the town's first newspaper, the *Nahuel Huapi*.
In the centre, Justo Jones, an Englishman, father of Zulema and Lesbia Jones. The man wearing a beret is Angel Roca, a landowner from Comallo. (Photo – Mange family collection, 1911.)

The first Commisson for Economic Development in Bariloche was set up on November 20th 1907. Members of the Commission were Luis Horn, Rubén Fernández and Federico (Friedrich) Reichert.
Standing next to the "historic cypress" is Francisco P. Moreno, accompanied by local authorities. (Photo – Labate family collection.)

J OSE Emanuel (Joseph Emmanuel) Vereertbrugghen, of Belgian origin, was the first doctor in San Carlos. He had to face severe epidemics of diphtheria at times when vaccine was not always available, and on one occasion Jarred Jones had to rush to Neuquén on horseback to get some. It is said that the doctor extracted teeth without pliers, using brute force and his bare fingers.

Anyone coming across him in the open would have taken him for a bandit by his untidy appearance, but he is remembered for his urbanity and gentleness, especially when playing sweet melodies on the grand piano in his home on lake Gutiérrez.

(Photo – Vereertbrugghen family collection)

Ernesto (Ernst) Schuhmacher, a baker, arrived in 1907 with his family and his aged father. (Photo – Schuhmacher family collection.)

The Gingins, Schmidt and Lamunière families. (Photo – Gingins family collection.)

Ernesto Schuhmacher (father). (Photo – Pablo Mange.)

Fabio Luelmo, the town's first pharmacist. (Photo – Luelmo family collection.)

BY its centenary year, 1910, San Carlos de Bariloche had a population of 1,250. There were still no roads, only car tracks, and no bridges; on the other hand the telegraph and postal systems were functioning, the latter by means of stages where fresh horses were available to cover the 105 leagues to Neuquén. There was a doctor in the village, and trade and business were thriving. Life was peaceful and harmonious, but much remained to be done. With imagination, strength and hard work the town continued to develop and incorporate modern ideas into its daily routine.

View of the town, c. 1912. The building on the right was on the corner of what today are Mitre and Frey streets. (Photo – Frey family collection.)

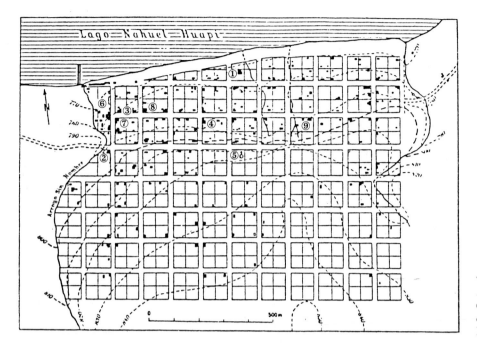

Town plan of Bariloche c. 1911. ① Police Station. ② Post Office. ③ School. ④ Forestry Commission. ⑤ Church. ⑥ Chile-Argentine company. ⑦ *Lahusen* store. ⑧ *Perito Moreno* Hotel. ⑨ *Swiss* Hotel. (Map by Emilio Frey.)

IN 1911 the census showed 197 buildings in the urban sector. The Chile-Argentine company was declining by now, and Primo Capraro bought up their premises. Don Primo was able to count on the support of several immigrant families, and through faith and hard work he was able to construct an empire.

The old headquarters of the Chile-Argentine Cattle and Trading Company became home to a whole gamut of activities: fruit distribution, import-export, structural and rural carpentry, a sawmill, a foundry, a Ford agency, a boat yard, a YPF* agency, a news service for the *Patria Degli Italiani* newspaper, an Italian Consulate…

* *Yacimientos Petrolíferos Fiscales,* the Argentine state petroleum company.

The old *San Carlos* store, acquired by Primo Capraro. (Photo – Newbery family collection.)

AMONG the technicians on the Hydrological Studies Commission was a forestry engineer by the name of Max Rothkugel, who, in a report produced in 1916 entitled *Los Bosques Patagónicos* (The Patagonian Forests), gave a detailed analysis of forest fires during the summer 1913-14. Evidence indicated that these fires had been started intentionally and had been extinguished by fortuitous rains, which was just as well considering the limited resources of the small gangs of firefighters available to deal with them. The main cause of these fires seems to have been the clearing of woodland for agriculture or pasture.

View of the town taken from Frey Street, almost on the corner of Moreno Street, towards the west, 1913. (Photo – Hydrological Studies Commission.)

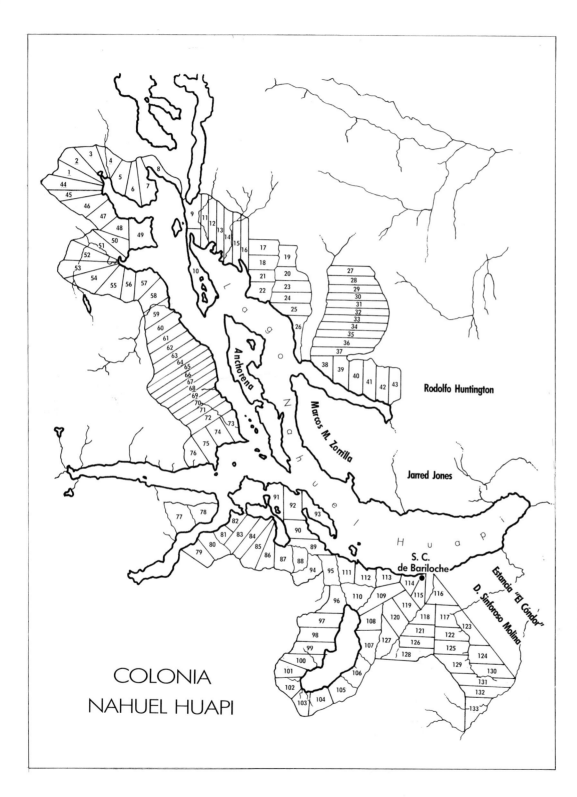

COLONIA
NAHUEL HUAPI

THE Nahuel Huapi colony was slow to attract settlers, who showed little interest in establishing themselves there, and was mainly pasture land, suitable for cattle. It was subdivided into agricultural lots of 625 hectares and small holdings of 40 or 50 hectares.

The Swiss residents gathered around lake Moreno and its environs, in the area which became to be known as *Colonia Suiza*, or the Swiss Colony. Jacinto Giménez —the only veteran of the Nahuel Huapi campaign to have obtained land in the region in recognition of his services— farmed cattle in pasture lot 116, while in lot 118 Fernando (Ferdinando) Pizzuti had dug a limestone quarry and in 41 Pablo Mange had planted apple trees and was attempting to produce cider.

Other settlers included Otto Goedecke, in lot 39, Luis Pefaure, in 40, Benito Boock, in 42, Tomás (Thomas) Wharton, in 43, Juan (John) O'Connor, in 44, Camilo (Camille) Goye, in 83, Enrique (Henry) Felley, in 84 and Félix Goye, in 85.

In time, as both the town and the national park expanded their limits, much of this agricultural colony disappeared.

THE schooner *Pampa* was built in 1913 by the engineer Otto Mühlenpfordt, at the request of Aarón de Anchorena.

Although finely finished and streamlined the ship was not a success, as the winds which blow almost incessantly on lake Nahuel Huapi are unfavourable to navigation by sail.

Mühlenpfordt, who had reassembled the steamboat *Cóndor* for Wiederhold, also constructed other boats, such as the sailboat *Venus*, for Conrado (Konrad) Eggers and the *Selckt*, the *Estrella* and the steamer *Cachirulo* for Primo Capraro. All these ships proudly sailed on Nahuel Huapi.

Aarón de Anchorena set up a timber industry on Victoria island, and introduced exotic animal species there, such as deer from the northern hemisphere, with the idea of setting up game reserves for hunting. He also stocked the area with pheasants, principally for decorative purposes.

The schooner *Pampa*, 1913. (Photo – Frey family collection.)

(Photo – Capraro family collection.)

THE town was growing, and some old houses were now being replaced by bigger and more comfortable ones. The old houses were not pulled down however, just moved.

Santiago Castillo made a career out of this rather unusual profession. He used jacks to raise houses from their foundations and inserted rollers beneath. With the help of oxen the houses were then dragged to their new location, no matter how far away that might be, and this was done so smoothly that the move was often effected without even removing the furniture.

If the journey was long the inhabitants of the house would continue to live in it during the move, and Castillo would connect up the electricity to the nearest outlet as they stopped for the night.

One move which is still remembered is that of the Bureau of Lands and Colonies offices, housed in a two storey building which was moved from the corner of Moreno and Villegas streets to that of Elflein and Morales.

Castillo's speciality was no longer feasible when oxen were replaced by tractors, as the vibrations and movements of the heavy machines caused structural damage to the buildings, making such moves impossible.

(Photo – Modesto Fernández Seijo.)

THE first motor cars arrived in the village in 1912. Three Mercedes Benz automobiles, as big as threshing machines, brought the Governor of Neuquén, don Eduardo Elordi, and Francisco P. Moreno, in his capacity as President of the reception committee for Theodore Roosevelt, who was passing through Bariloche as a tourist on his way to Chile.

These cars remained in the hands of the local authorities, being used for postal deliveries and official transport. The first private motor car in Bariloche was a Ford belonging to Jarred Jones.

Pilcaniyeu Viejo, 1916, in front of the *Giménez* Hotel. This group of police officers and agents of the neighbouring areas was searching for prisoners who had escaped from the prison at Fort Roca. (Photo – Cejas family collection.)

WITH the intention of stimulating regional development, the Minister of Public Works, Ezequiel Ramos Mejía, contracted the North American geologist Bailey Willis, asking him to form a team to analyze the possibilities of developing North Patagonia. Out of this arose the Hydrological Studies Commission, founded in 1911. Bailey Willis was the Director of this commission, and his chief assistant was Emilio Frey, an engineer appointed for his comprehensive knowledge of the region.

First they made plans for the provision of drinking water at San Antonio. They then started laying a railway line up to Nahuel Huapi, originally planned as an international line, and studied the various border passes and communications with the north and south of Argentina.

They looked into the possibilities of founding residential districts in San Carlos de Bariloche, of promoting

tourism in the San Pedro peninsula, of constructing a hotel on the top of mount Runge and establishing an industrial estate on the higher reaches of the river Limay, along its left bank. This last project would have included building a dam on the river, at a location known as *Anfiteatro*, to convert the first few kilometres of the Limay into a lake and make this navigable as far as the projected city. Turbines would also have been incorporated into the dam to provide electricity for industry.

The project was approved, plans were drawn up and streets were even laid out on the chosen site. But the time was not right; the situation changed and the industrial estate was never built.

The Hydrological Studies Commision in San Carlos de Bariloche, 1913. Also present is Dr. Vereertbrugghen (stroking the dog) and his wife (in the dark coat). In the centre is the geologist Bailey Willis. (Photo – Frey family collection.)

Inside the wagon-office in which the
Hydrological Studies Commission began its field
work, in Aguada Cecilio, 1911. (Photo – Emilio
Frey.)

Emilio Frey, Chief Assistant of the Hydrological Studies Commission.

María Rosa Schuhmacher de Frey shared her husband's outside life with the Hydrological Studies Commission. This photograph was taken on their honeymoon.

(Photos – Frey family collection.)

In the course of his field work, in 1912, Emilio Frey came across this group of men who were cutting a way for the railway. This line was not to reach San Carlos de Bariloche until several years later. (Photo – Emilio Frey.)

Opening up the way... (Photo – E. Frey.)

The first track… (Photo – E. Frey.)

Pupils at the German school in Bariloche, with their teachers, Enrique (Heinrich) Lührs and his wife, 1921. (Photo – Lührs family collection.)

Sirio-Lebanese immigrants arriving in 1917. Their journey had been arranged by the Lebanese Embassy. The group consisted of the Simón, Jalil, Manzur, Srur and Chamón families. (Photo – Lebanese Embassy archives.)

FRANCISCO Moreno's cypress was newly declared of historic importance in a ceremony at which the speakers were Armando Teobaldo Alizieri (Director of School N° 16), Primo Capraro and the schoolteacher, Carlos Modesto Castro, the last of whom brought a tear to the eyes of all those present with his oratorial skills. At the same time the street which passed by the tree was given the name of "Francisco P. Moreno". This was widely approved, especially by Primo Capraro, who from that day on never missed an opportunity at a public ceremony to name yet another of the town's streets.

Capraro was unaware –or perhaps unconcerned– that the law forbade streets to be named after living men and women. It is for this reason that the streets of Bariloche bear the names of so many townsfolk and characters of the time: Otto Goedecke, Emilio Morales, Ada María Elflein, Angel Gallardo, Horacio Anasagasti, Antonio Tiscornia, Domingo Fernández Beschtedt, Eduardo Elordi, Santiago Albarracín, León Quaglia and Clemente Onelli. Emilio Frey once returned from a journey to the capital to find that a street had been christened with his name, which annoyed him enormously.

But this kind of activity, commonly associated with Primo Capraro, was well received by the townspeople. A man of *brio*, he was inventive and imaginative, innocent and gentle. From an infinite stock of memories

School ceremony, 1921, at the foot of the "historic cypress", the town's natural monument. (Photo – Frey family collection.)

of him there is perhaps one which, although trivial, demonstrates his personality.

A Swiss family by name of Goye, who lived by lake Moreno, were expecting a child and Don Primo was to be the godfather. At the time the First World War had just broken out in Europe, and brothers and friends of this Swiss couple were set against each other. Capraro was disturbed by this sad turn of events, and, filled with the hope and happiness which a newly born child inspires, chose for the infant the Christian name "Neutral". And so, in San Carlos de Bariloche, there grew up a man with the name of Neutral Goye, a living and walking example of the indomitable spirit of these pioneers.

MARTIN Sheffield was a legendary character. A North American, he arrived in San Carlos at the turn of the century and worked as a cattle driver. He also tried unsuccessfully to make his fortune panning for gold. Although a peaceful man by nature he had a passion for firearms, and was said to have been able to shoot a lighted cigarette out of a person's mouth. A loudmouth and drunkard, he was well known throughout the bars of the area for his tall tales and the impossible feats he claimed.

One of his exploits reached the ears of the whole country and even beyond its borders. What happened is that one day Sheffield wrote a letter to his family in the States, somewhat exaggerating the natural beauty of the region, telling them that there were animals in Patagonia that were over ten metres tall. On receiving this news his alarmed relatives showed the letter to the director of a museum, and the latter began enquiries which were soon to reach the ears of the general public. Before very long, the international press, natural science museums, the Buenos Aires Zoo, the Society for the Protection of Animals and diplomats from both countries were embroiled in the affair. A North American ex-president wondered how much

Martin Sheffield (Photo – Sheffield family collection.)

truth there was in the story; in Buenos Aires a tango called *El Plesiosaurio* was written, and some enterprising individuals even manufactured and sold pencils in the shape of this prehistoric animal.

The director of the Buenos Aires Zoo, Clemente Onelli, was sceptical, but bowing to the enormous pressure exerted by the press and public opinion was obliged to organise an expedition to the alleged dinosaur's homeland. Sheffield took care to lie low for a while.

Clemente Onelli. (Photo – Patagonian Museum.)

DURING the 1922 Carnival the much vaunted plesiosaurus burst onto the streets of Bariloche, built by Primo Capraro and is followers. Some days before, the Zoo's investigatory commission, led by Clemente Onelli, had been informed that: *An old Indian witchdoctor has predicted that the plesiosaurus will appear in the streets of Bariloche next Tuesday.*

And so it did, even if science has not yet been able to classify Sheffield's animal.

(Photo – Enrique Lührs.)

(Photo – Rafael Soriani.)

The corner of Moreno and Villegas streets. In
the foreground, the old police station; behind,
the Banco Nación building, inaugurated in
1922; opposite, the Castro's family home;
behind, the *Spalato* bar; on the left, the *Lahusen*
warehouses. (Photo – Enrique Lührs.)

Mitre street in 1922. From left to right: the
Gingins home; the Mange home; School N° 16
(the building belonged to the rancher Fermín
Salaberry, who lent it to the school); on the
corner of Rolando Street, the *Los Lagos* Hotel,
at that time owned by the Garza family. In the
background, fields being prepared for sowing in
what today is the district of Belgrano.
(Photo – Enrique Lührs.)

(Photo – Enrique Lührs.)

DON Carlos Wiederhold, who lived in Puerto Varas, in Chile, corresponded with many of his friends in Bariloche. When Primo Capraro heard of Wiederhold's intention to settle permanently in Santiago he organised a banquet for the first inhabitant of what was now the town centre. Wiederhold was invited to attend, and his arrival eagerly awaited by the oldest families. The banquet took place on February 8th 1925, a country lunch on the Runge property. Wiederhold was presented with a commemorative parchment and speeches were made by Primo Capraro and Pedro Alcoba Pitt.

Wiederhold can be seen in the photograph wearing a bowler hat and smoking a cigar, no doubt a gift, and surrounded by, amongst others, the Boock, Pefaure, Capraro, Frey, Crespo, Runge, Hagemann, Goedecke, Jung, Agundez, Panozzi, Márquez, Vera, Rothschildberger, Winckler, Gingins, Suárez and Pizzuti families.

Parchment given to Carlos Wiederhold in 1925, as a sign of respect and good will from the townsfolk to the first settler in what is now the urban centre of the city. The artwork is by the painter Américo Panozzi. The text refers to the thirtieth anniversary of the foundation of San Carlos de Bariloche. In fact Wiederhold set up the *San Carlos* store in 1895 but the town was established legally in 1902. The parchment is now hanging in the Mayor's office in Bariloche.

FOR many years San Carlos de Bariloche lacked a police force to safeguard its people and their property. These were still times of bandits, and the possibility of night attacks on townsfolk and their homes something that was always at the back of people's minds.

Fearful gangs of North American *bandoleros* roamed Patagonia during the early part of the century. Bank raids in Río Gallegos in 1905, Villa Mercedes in 1907 and a botched bank raid in San Julián alternated with attacks on homesteads, businessmen and travellers.

Everyone knew the names of the Wilson Brothers, Place, Evans, Harry Logan, Duff –alias Gold Tooth– and Ryan, the last of these supposedly the name used by Butch Cassidy, who travelled around in the company of his lady friend, Ethel Rose.

In those times any stranger was treated with suspicion, just in case, which caused not a few cases of confusion. Stories grew around these instances, their veracity often varying according to the imagination of the narrator...

In Bariloche itself one was never quite sure if these individuals had committed any crime, but this was not the case in the outlying settlements. Public alarm reached a peak when a store owned by a man called Palavecino was attacked in Epuyén, and this moved the settlers to call for police reinforcements.

In response, almost 300 border police arrived from Chubut, under the command of Major Mateo Gebhardt, and from Río Negro, under Adrián del Busto. Working together, they concentrated on the area of the border passes around the river Manso. However, unfamiliar with the region or its inhabitants, they acted summarily, and many settlers were arrested and taken to Bolsón or Bariloche to be interrogated. Some spent as much as a year in custody before being set free. From that time onwards a detachment of these fierce policemen was to stay in Bariloche.

Chubut border police, photographed in Sunica, to the south of Esquel, 1913. (Photo – *Esquel* newspaper archives.)

THIS was the first public motor transport to run between Neuquén and Bariloche, covering the 500 kilometres in a mere 38 hours.

The ony snag was, as a notice warned the public: *Timetable subject to alteration without previous warning.*

It was quite usual to find this car owned by the Jones and Suárez company, a Buick driven by Amaranto Suárez, stuck in the sandbanks along the way.

Amaranto Suárez and his Buick. (Photo – Neuquén History Museum.)

Advertisement from a Neuquén newspaper, 1916.

The roads had their problems...

A driver and his companion stop for a mate.

Travelling from Pilcaniyeu to Bariloche, 1925.

(Photos – Mange family collection.)

(Photos – Mange family collection.)

THE first cinema in Bariloche was owned by the Parsons Brothers, and opened in 1917 on the corner of Mitre and Frey streets. The whole town was enthralled with the romanticism of silent cinema. As there was only one projector the show was interrupted each time the reel had to be changed; at these times the cinema became a bar as well. Films were changed once a month and continued to be shown as long as there was a public to watch them. They say it was better to go and see the film after the third showing or so, as by then the operator's assistant –usually a small boy– would have learned to manipulate the story boards (which kept the public informed about what was happening or being said in the film), so that they coincided with what was actually taking place on the screen.

(Photo – Frey family collection.)

Winter 1923. The tall building was the Boock store, situated on what is now Mitre 550. There was a power generator here and, as there were no metres at the time, people were charged according to the number of lamps they had installed in their homes. The generator was later to burn down and the town was left in darkness for several years. (Photo – National Archives.)

May 25th celebrations, 1915. On national holidays people would celebrate in the main street of the town, taking part in running races, games of chance and all kinds of local sports. A barbecue was held in the meadow by the old Police Station and was attended by all the townsfolk and officials.

The photograph shows the corner of Mitre and Fernández Beschtedt streets. The house on the left was the pharmacy, assiduously tended by Fabio Luelmo. (Photo – Frey family collection.)

One of the three "Federal" lorries used by Manuel Castro to start up his freight business. All in all he was not successful, not least because of the precarious nature of the roads in the area, which at times made transport very hazardous. (Photo – Enrique Lührs.)

The corner of Mitre and Rolando streets, winter 1916. In the foreground, the house belonging to José Luis Pefaure, first Justice of the Peace in the Department of Bariloche. In the centre, the parish church, inaugurated in 1908 by Father Zacarías Genghini. On the right, the "historic cypress", under whose shade civic and scholastic functions took place. (Photo – National Archives.)

Bellevue Hotel, built by Santiago Castillo, situated on Moreno and Rolando streets.

The Márquez family home.

PRIMO Capraro, owner of the most important sawmill in the region, who with the support of fellow countrymen specialised in different aspects of building, built nearly all of the houses in the town and its surroundings during the 20s.

At heart Capraro was a builder, but in most cases he looked after the overall organisation and planning of the work, leaving his foreman, Santiago Castillo, to deal with the actual construction.

Generally the owners gave little more than the general idea of what kind of house they required and Castillo supplied the rest, with the instinctive flair he had acquired in his native Chile. In the earlier days they built mainly with *alerce* or cypress tiles, but when the mill was mechanised it became more common to build with overlapping boards.

Brick was little used, becoming more common towards the end of the decade. Building with rubblework was much more expensive, and there were few who could afford it in Bariloche. There were brick ovens in the upper stretches of the creek where the Margaritas district is today. Bricks were made by the Debarba family, and there was a limestone quarry near the Carbón hill, run by the Pizzuti family since the beginning of the century.

(Photos – Capraro family collection.)

THE Pefaure family home stood on the corner of Mitre and Palacios streets. The house, built of wooden tiles, was constructed at the beginning of the century and was acquired by José Luis Pefaure in 1910. Originally much smaller, it was elarged in the same style.

Only three architecturally similar houses were built, all constructed between 1903 and 1905. The style is that of the German colonies in the south of Chile, and these houses were possibly the work of Adolfo (Adolf) Billike.

(Photo – Pefaure family collection.)

The Banco Nación building, inaugurated in 1922, stood on the corner of Mitre and Villegas streets. It was built by Primo Capraro to plans designed by Peralta, Martínez and Denis, Buenos Aires architects who sent the blueprints down to Bariloche. (Photo – Enrique Lührs.)

El Parque boarding house, c. 1920 (Photo –
Lührs family collection.)

Main house, *Tequel Malal* estancia, property of
Jarred Jones. (Photo – Gingins family
collection.)

Main house, *El Cóndor* estancia, built by Primo
Capraro. (Photo – Capraro family collection.)

Lahusen store, built on Mitre and Quaglia
streets in 1911. (Photo – Gingins family
collection.)

A civic function in front of the *Swiss* Hotel. In the foreground can be seen the band which Capraro started after he returned from a visit to a religious school in Buenos Aires. In a corner of the school he found a number of musical instruments which no one was using, managed to persuade the school authorities to let him have them, and then used them to set up this band, in which everyone who knew how to played. Half of the musicians came from the Soriany family.

(Photo – Enrique Lührs.)

Bariloche cemetery, 1927. (Photo – National Archives.)

Bariloche port and Capraro's sawmill. In 1924 a fire completely destroyed the mill, which stood on the site of today's Civic Centre. It was a severe setback for Capraro but with the help of his employees he managed to get the business back to normal in record time. (Photos – Capraro family collection.)

1923

1927

IN the 20s a small fleet of steamers navigated the lake, all the property of Primo Capraro and at the service of the tourist agencies Exprinter and Villalonga. Tourists were offered transport to Correntoso, Puerto Tigre and Victoria Island, and an international service was available by way of Peulla, in combination with Ricardo (Richard) Roth's Andina del Sud company. Also the steamer *Cóndor* sailed round the perimeter of Lake Nahuel Huapi, carrying supplies for the settlers.

It was quite normal for a whole football team and their families to sail to Campanario in order to play a match, and not at all unusual to find people sailing at night to some social gathering: a dance, perhaps, in Conrado Molina's estancia.

The *Cóndor*, under the permanent command of Daniel Márquez, provided assistance and security to lakeside dwellers who were otherwise cut off by the cruel winter snows.

Otto Mühlenpfordt built four steamers for Capraro; *Estrella*, *Gavilán*, *Nahuel Huapi I* and *Nahuel Huapi II* –the last of these renamed *Cachirulo* (in English "pot"), on account of the awkward way it handled– not to mention half a dozen smaller boats.

(Photos – Capraro family collection.)

The steamboat *Gavilán*, the launch *Halcón* and the steamer *Nahuel Huapi*.

The steamboat *Nahuel Huapi II* or *Cachirulo*.

The steamboat *Cóndor*.

97

Bariloche port. In the foreground a launch belonging to the Neuquén Government for official use and at the service of those in the neighbourhood by request. To arrange for its use it was only necessary to pay a small sum to the captain and provide him with two or three cans of fuel, according to the distance to be covered. (Photos – Capraro family collection.)

The steamer *Nahuel Huapi*.

The port at López bay. Notice the steamer *Patagonia*, belonging to the Ministry of Public Works and Services. This ship proved unseaworthy and was withdrawn from service after very few voyages. It was subsequently run aground on the beach and converted into the *El Barquito* tea shop. (Photo – Frey family collection.)

Puerto Tigre.

(Photos – Capraro family collection.)

IN a decree of April 8th 1922, countersigned by President Hipólito Yrigoyen and his Minister of Agriculture, Honorio Pueyrredón, the first official limits of the National Southern Park were defined at an area of 785.000 hectares. Article 5 of the decree entrusted the administration and control of the park to the engineer and geographer of the Lands Bureau, Emilio Frey.

This official action was paralleled by a private initiative, embodied in the Commission in favour of the National Southern Park, later to be recognised by the national government in a decree of President Alvear on April 14th, 1924, endorsed by Minister Tomás Le Breton.

The first six park wardens, men carefully picked by Emilio Frey, commenced work in January 1928. Frey also set out a list of rules, a copy of which –belonging to the Andrés Beros collection– appears on this page. Subsequent commissions in favour of the National Southern Park were presided over by Manuel A. Montes de Oca, Angel Gallardo and Exequiel Bustillo.

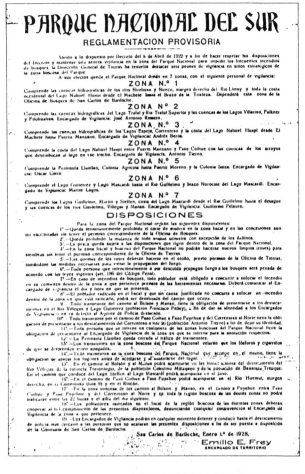

Primo Capraro, owner of the Hotel *Correntoso*, accompanying a group of tourists, among whom can be seen Dr. Angel Gallardo (with white hair). (Photo – Lührs family collection.)

Police and civilians in search of the La Lipela bandits. (Photo – Newbery family collection.)

IN 1928 a fearful band of murderers terrorised the region, lead by a certain Roberto Foster Rojas, or as the newspapers named him for his blood thirsty crimes, the La Lipela jackal. He was aided and abetted by two accomplices who went by the names of Román and Puchi.

A posse of police and civilians set out in search of these bandits. Among the police were officer Mauro Licardi and agents Duarte, Delgado and Villalón; the civilians included Teodosio Ruiz, Justo Daract, Said Andem and Vicente Bustos.

The miscreants were surrounded in the Los Repollos river and after a fierce shootout, in which Puchi died and Román was wounded, Foster Rojas gave himself up. In the place where they had been fighting they found seven hundred spent cartridge cases and another seventy-four unused bullets.

Roberto Foster Rojas caught and bound, photographed outside the Bariloche Police Station. (Photo – Hernández family collection.)

A distinguished visitor aboard the steamboat *Cóndor*, North American Army General John Joseph Pershing, seen here lighting a cigar. With him are Captain Pujol (left) and Otto Mühlenpfordt. Pershing was a guest of Aarón de Anchorena on Victoria Island. He fought against Pancho Villa in Mexico, participated in the secession of Texas from Mexico and served as a North American General in the First World War. (Photo – Emilio Frey.)

Homage to members of the desert expedition: inauguration of the memorial monument at the foot of mount Villegas. April 3rd 1928. In the centre of the picture, General Antonio Tiscornia; on the far right, naval captain Santiago Albarracín. (Photo – Enrique Lührs.)

The Prince of Wales and the Duke of Kent –Edward and George of the House of Windsor-, sons of King George V, visited Bariloche in 1930. Edward succeeded his father to the throne as Edward VIII; his brother died in a flying accident in the Second World War. The photograph was taken in the doorway of the Banco Nación. (Photo – Garza family collection.)

101

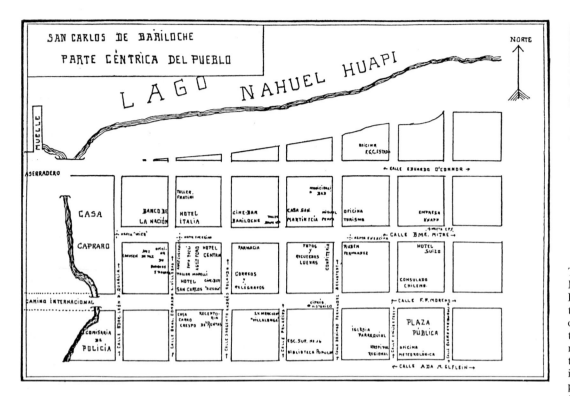

MAPA
DEL
NAHUEL HUAPI
Y
PARQUE NACIONAL DEL SUD
EDITADO POR LA
OFICINA DE TURISMO
DE
HILDEBRANDT y MEILING
EN
SAN CARLOS DE BARILOCHE

TURISMO

SAN CARLOS DE BARILOCHE
1930/31

Es Propiedad

Title page and plan from Hildebrandt and Meiling's tourist brochure. Otto Meiling came to Bariloche in 1930. At first he spent his time in the tourist trade, but because of his great love of the mountains he devoted more and more time to skiing and climbing. He was a founder member of the Bariloche Andean Club, started the first ski school and opened the first factory in the country to manufacture skis. Skis produced at this factory were sold under the trade name *Tronador*, after the highest mountain in the region. Meiling was an indefatigable walker and climber, scaling nearly all the peaks in the area, and gave most of the mountains their present day names. He donated all his belongings to his beloved club, amongst them the mountain hut which he had built on mount Otto. Mount Otto, incidentally, is not named after him but after Otto Goedecke. Meiling climbed mount Tronador (3,354m) for the last time on his eightieth birthday.

In 1916 priests of the Salesian order opened a first aid station in Bariloche. This was situated behind the chapel they had built, in a building made available by the Mancioli family. It was here that Dr. Ernesto Serigós performed the first operation for appendicitis in San Carlos de Bariloche. The town's first hospital opened in 1930, on the corner of Mitre and Onelli streets. (Photo – Depellegrin family collection.)

102

Corner of Frey and Moreno Streets, 1930.
(Photo – Enrique Lührs.)

TRACK laying for the railways progressed very slowly. In 1911 the line reached Aguada Cecilio; in 1917 Ingeniero Jacobacci, and in 1929 it arrived at Pilcaniyeu. In order to reach Bariloche, passengers had to continue by road, a truly uncomfortable journey of some 70 kilometres. There was no bridge across the Pichi Leufu river, which therefore had to be forded. In the winter they carried thick boards on the roofs of the cars to help them negotiate the muddier parts of the road. Two firms, Reinaldo Knapp and Juan Frattini, offered transport between Bariloche and the end of the line.

Bridging the La Viuda gulch, 1930. The sleepers which are visible in the photo were later covered by a reinforcing embankment.

The Capraro Company was one of the leading firms contracted for the construction of these stretches of line, and was recognised especially for its skill in track-laying. Both the company's financial position and Primo Capraro's spirits were weakened as a result of long delays in payment.

(Photos – Capraro family collection.)

Primo Capraro poses with his children, c. 1930. (Photo – Capraro family collection.)

Inside Primo Capraro s store, 1924. (Photo – Depellegrin family collection.)

PRIMO Capraro committed suicide on October 4th 1932. He was a man of the Cordillera, considered by many of those who knew him as an archetype of the region. But he was more than that –he was essentially an Italian, and, like his ancestors, wherever he installed himself he became, through his innate sense of civilisation, a conqueror of deserts, a builder of cities and a layer of roads.

The bronze statue which bears his image in the Bariloche Civic Centre pays homage to his pioneer spirit, and was erected with contributions from the whole town.

(Photo from the booklet published by the Primo Capraro Homage Committee, Bariloche, 1934.)

THE first locomotive, trailing three passenger wagons, puffed and hooted its way into Bariloche in 1934, and the Buenos Aires - Bariloche service was inaugurated in December of the same year.

With this important rail link the people of the village were immediately to benefit from improved communications, transport and commercial possibilities.

(Photo – Archives of *La Nación* newspaper.)

Mitre Street, Winter 1935. (Photo – Lührs family collection.)

Photograph of what was then called the international route, now E. Bustillo Avenue, taken between Bariloche and Llao Llao, on the Bonita beach, c. 1930. (Photo – Ricardo Vallmitjana collection.)

Detail from an estate agent's publicity brochure. Different companies sliced the land up in ever smaller lots with no thought for the future consequences. In 1980 it was calculated that enough land within the municipal boundaries had been divided into lots to provide shelter for a million people.

The *La Gloria* chalet was constructed by Osvaldo (Oswald) Lauersdorf in 1929. Undeniably picturesque, it was the only building of its kind. (Photo – R. Vallmitjana collection.)

Label from a bottle of *Parque Nacional* beer, made in Bariloche by Zufiaur and Leberle with hops from the region. The brand name reflects the hope of the inhabitants for the development of the National Park and the implied touristic possibilities. (Iván Jara collection.)

107

LAW 12,103 was sanctioned by Congress on October 9th 1934, creating the National Parks Service, and the future of the park, thus given its present day name of Nahuel Huapi National Park, was guaranteed. This law was based on plans made by the geologist Bailey Willis, when he was working on the Hydrological Studies Commission, and was drawn up by Dr. Exequiel Bustillo.

This was a moment of great fulfillment. Bustillo, appointed President of the National Parks Service, possessed enormous drive and was well placed socially and politically, which was a great help to him in his task.

The policy of the national parks at that time was to encourage tourism as a means of improving the regional economy, and public works were considered the most important instruments of development in Argentina in the 1930s. It was these two ideas that spurred Bustillo into action.

The Park Superintendent, Emilio Frey, received enthusiastic letters from his President...

I should especially like to ask you to give the greatest attention possible to all the work now being started. The prompt and felicitous realisation of these tasks will to a great extent determine the future prestige of our division... you are Head of the park by appointment; may you also be so in fact, permanently translating our wishes into action, and endowing these works with the impetus with which we are inspired...

Everything remained to be done in Nahuel Huapi National Park. The first priority was a large hotel, and work started immediately on the construction of *Llao Llao*, a building of wood and stone conceived by the architect Alejandro Bustillo, and magnificently suited to the beauty of its location. Forty thousand wooden logs, cut from the nearby woods, were used in its construction. The hotel opened in 1938 and less than a year later, on October 29th 1939, it was destroyed in a disastrous fire.

At the same time the small town of San Carlos de Bariloche, which at that time had less than 4,000 inhabitants, was being transformed. The town was enlarged towards the west, running water was provided as well as sewerage, and a Civic Centre –based on plans by the architect Ernesto Estrada and officially opened in March 1939– was built to house the municipal offices, post office, police station, customs offices, tax offices, law courts, museum and library. The centre was completed by the National Parks building, built some one hundred metres from the square. The main streets of the town were asphalted and street lighting was improved, the style of the lamps being chosen to blend in with these new buildings.

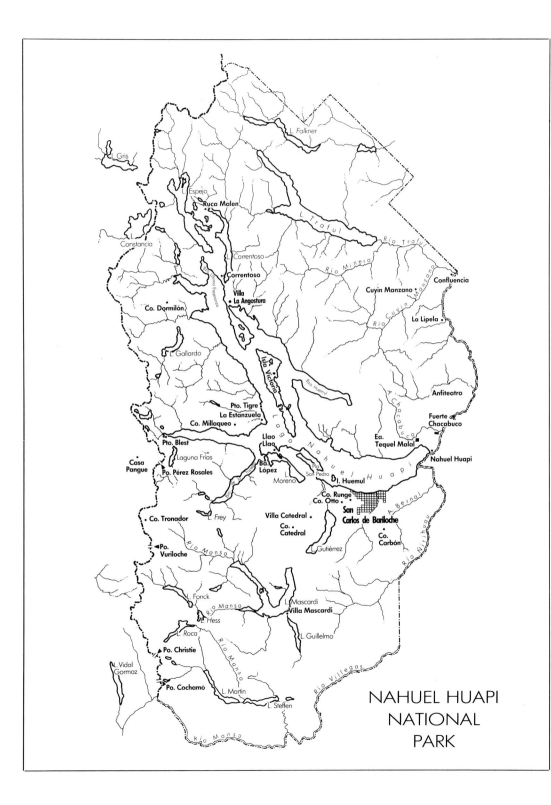

NAHUEL HUAPI
NATIONAL
PARK

The *Llao Llao* Hotel, opened in 1938. (Photo –
G. Kaltschmidt.)

Destroyed by fire in 1939. (Photo – W. Furst.)

The German school, being visited by a similar school from the south of Chile, 1935. (Photo – Godofredo Kaltschmidt.)

EUROPEAN political crises were reflected in the wavering spirits of members of the different ethnic and national communities living in Bariloche. These distant events, every day less intelligible because of the time and distance which separated the immigrants from their former homelands, sometimes had strange repercussions.

The Capraro sawmill blew its whistle at midday to announce a rest period. Enrique (Heinrich) Lunde's boilers did exactly the same thing. But their respective clocks did not always keep the same time, and sometimes their signals were noticeably out of phase. This albeit trivial matter confused the populace, as many businessmen raised or lowered their shutters on hearing the whistle. As time went by some –according to their nationalities– began to follow one whistle or the other. People began to talk of *Italian time* and *German time*, and those who had no truck with old world problems muttered ironically about neighbours who couldn't even agree on the time of day.

Over the years and generations ethnic bonds loosened, if they did not perhaps altogether disappear, and assumed the role of distinctive signs of a new, pluralist society whose members preserved many of the traditions and customs of their old countries.

THE National Park authorities brought ski champion and instructor Hans Nöbl out from Switzerland to study the possibility of opening a winter sports centre in Bariloche. After considering various alternatives, one of them being the Dormilón, they decided to locate the ski slopes on the mount Catedral. The National Parks ski school opened in 1938 under European instructors, and another, with local instructors, was soon underway. Among these were Camilo Pefaure, Antonio Depellegrin, Armando Denaghi and Ernesto Schuhmacher.

National Parks provided basic amenities at the foot of the slopes and built a shelter near the peak, later to be christened the Antonio Lynch shelter. Construction work was also started to accommodate a cable car ordered from Italy, but this was not put into use until 1950 as its manufacture was interrupted by the war. A complementary ski lift was installed on the upper slopes, and two "Peters" snow-sweepers were brought in to keep the roads clear.

(Photos – Modesto Fernández Seijo.)

Leading this ascent of the Catedral slopes is the Swiss ski champion and instructor Hans Nöbl, 1938.

End of a ski race, Catedral, 1938.

THE State Air Line, Líneas Aéreas del Estado, inaugurated a regular passenger service between Buenos Aires and Bariloche on September 4th 1940, using three-engined Junker aircraft which put down at Santa Rosa and Neuquén. As from May 14th 1947, the flights were taken over by Aeroposta Argentina, later to become Aerolíneas Argentinas.

(Photo – *La Prensa* newspaper archives.)

Winter 1939; children take advantage of the slope on Rolando Street. (Photo – Modesto Fernández Seijo.)

TO improve navigation on Lake Nahuel Huapi, the National Park authorities brought the motorboat *Modesta Victoria*, the most elegant vessel yet to grace these waters. Landing stages were also constructed where necessary.

Bariloche port, c. 1952. (Photo – Augusto Vallmitjana.)

Looking from the Civic Centre down Mitre Street, towards the west, 1939. (Photo – Modesto Fernández Seijo.)

Llao Llao Hotel, reconstructed after the fire and reopened on New Year's Day, 1940. (Photo – Augusto Vallmitjana.)

Mitre Street, c. 1950. (Photo – Modesto Fernández Seijo.)

IN order to consolidate the development of the National Park a fish-breeding station was opened and a forestry nursery established on Victoria island. Towards the end of the 30s a considerable network of roads had been laid down, offering scenic views to the tourist, and these, with their inevitable bridges, made it possible to reach the most remote spots of the region, as well as the recently founded tourist villages at the foot of the Catedral slopes, in the Llao Llao peninsula, on the Mascardi and Traful lakes and in Angostura. Chapels were also built in the villages of Catedral, Llao Llao and Angostura, and a much larger Gothic style church, designed by Alejandro Bustillo, was erected in Bariloche on the coastal avenue. Accommodation for tourists was provided in hotels at Catedral, at Ruca Malén, in Puerto Blest, in the Frías lake, and in the vicinity of López bay. Camping sites were provided on Bonita beach and on the Huemul inlet. With the local people in mind a regional hospital was built, as well as the D. F. Sarmiento school (today School Nº 266), and the Ricardo Gutiérrez Children's Home.

Tourist buses belonging to the International Company of Motor Transport (CITA) at the foot of mount Tronador, 1942. (Photo – Modesto Fernández Seijo.)

1940. (Photo – Modesto Fernández Seijo.)

(Photo – Modesto Fernández Seijo.)

BARILOCHE in the fifties.
Francisco Moreno's dream
slowly became reality: a National
Park for the enjoyment of
generations present and to come.
Bariloche has come to embody the
efforts of all those pioneers, men
and women, who together planted
the seeds of a privileged city that
their children would one day
inherit.

The 50s.

The 60s.

(Photos – Augusto Vallmitjana.)

118

May 1987. (Photo – Ricardo Vallmitjana.)

BIBLIOGRAPHY

Albarracín, Santiago. *Estudios generales sobre los ríos Negro, Limay y Collón Cura, y lago de Nahuel Huapi*. Buenos Aires, 1886.

Amunátegui, Miguel Luis. *La cuestión de límites entre Chile y la República Argentina*. Santiago, 1881.

Anchorena, Aarón de. *Descripción geográfica de la Patagonia y valles andinos*. Buenos Aires, 1902.

Arce, José. *La cuestión de límites con Chile*. Buenos Aires, 1965.

Artayeta, Enrique Amadeo. *Biografía del perito Francisco P. Moreno*, National Parks Annals, I:1-26. Buenos Aires, 1945.

Barros, Alvaro. *Indios, fronteras y seguridad interior*, new edition of writings by Col. Barros. Buenos Aires, 1975.

Barros, Alvaro. *Fronteras y territorios federales de las pampas del sud*. Buenos Aires, 1872.

Barros Arana, Diego. *La cuestión de límites entre Chile y la República Argentina*. Santiago, 1898.

Bertomeu, Carlos A. *El perito Moreno, centinela de la Patagonia*. Buenos Aires, 1949.

Biedma, José Juan. *Crónica histórica del Río Negro de Patagones (1774-1843)*. Buenos Aires, 1905.

Biedma, Juan Martín. *Toponimia del parque nacional Nahuel Huapi*. Buenos Aires, 1967.

Biedma, Juan Martín. *Crónica histórica del lago Nahuel Huapi*. Buenos Aires, 1987.

Bourne, Benjamin F. *The Giants of Patagonia; Captain Bourne's Account of his Captivity amongst the Extraordinary Savages of Patagonia*. London, 1853.

Bulnes, Gonzalo. *Chile y Argentina, un debate de 55 años*. Santiago, 1898.

Bustillo, Exequiel. *El despertar de Bariloche*. Buenos Aires, 1971.

Cabrera, Angel L. *Origen y evolución de la flora del parque nacional Nahuel Huapi*, Anales de Parques Nacionales IV:43-53. Buenos Aires, 1954.

De Augusta, F.J. *Diccionario araucano-español*. Santiago, 1966.

De Moesbach, E.W. *Idioma mapuche*. Santiago, 1966.

Doering, Adolfo, y Lorentz, Pablo. *La conquista del desierto. Diario de los miembros de la comisión científica de la expedición de 1879*. Buenos Aires, 1939.

Ebélot, Alfred. *La expedición al río Negro*, original article in *Revue des Deux Mondes*, Paris, 1/5/1880, translated into spanish as A. Ebélot, *Relatos de la frontera*. Buenos Aires, 1968.

Eriksen, Wolfgang. *Kolonisation und Tourismus in Ostpatagonien*. Bonn, 1970.

Erize, Esteban. *Diccionario comentado mapuche-español*. Buenos Aires, 1960.

Erize, Francisco, et al. *Los parques nacionales de la Argentina*. Madrid, 1981.

Espinosa, Antonio. *La conquista del desierto. Diario del capellán de la expedición de 1879*. Buenos Aires, 1939.

Fernández, Jorge. *Restos de embarcaciones primitivas en el lago Nahuel Huapi*, Anales de Parques Nacionales, XIV:45-77. Buenos Aires, 1978.

Fonck, Francisco. *Viajes de Fray Francisco Menéndez a Nahuel Huapi*. Valparaíso, 1900.

Furlong, Guillermo. *Vida apostólica y glorioso martirio del venerable P. Nicolás Mascardi*, Anales de Parques Nacionales, I:195-236. Buenos Aires, 1945.

Hasbrouck, A. *The conquest of the desert*, Hispanic American Historical Review, XV, 2:195-228. Durham, 1935.

Holdich, Thomas H. *The Countries of the Kings's Award*. London, 1904.

Holdich, Thomas H. *Political Frontiers and Boundary Making*. London, 1916.

Lupo, Remigio. *Conquista del desierto*. Buenos Aires, 1938.

Ministerio de Guerra. *Expedición al gran lago Nahuel Huapi. Partes y documentos. Anexo a la memoria de Guerra*. Buenos Aires, 1881.

Ministerio de Guerra. *Informe de la Comisión Científica agregada al Estado Mayor General de la expedición al Río Negro*. Buenos Aires, 1879.

Moreno, Eduardo. *Reminiscencias de Francisco P. Moreno*. Buenos Aires, 1942.

Moreno, Francisco P. *Apuntes preliminares sobre una excursión a los territorios del Neuquén, Río Negro, Chubut y Santa Cruz*, Revista del Museo de La Plata, VIII:199-372. La Plata, 1897.

Moreno, Francisco P. *Viaje a la Patagonia septentrional*, Anales de la Sociedad Científica Argentina, I:182-197. Buenos Aires, 1876.

Musters, George C. *At Home with the Patagonians*. London, 1871.

O'Connor, Eduardo. *Exploración del alto Limay y del lago Nahuel Huapi*, Boletín del Instituto Geográfico Argentino, V:232-264. Buenos Aires, 1884.

Olascoaga, Manuel. *Estudio topográfico de La Pampa y Río Negro*, second edition. Buenos Aires, 1974.

Pedersen, Asbjorn. *Las pinturas rupestres del parque nacional Nahuel Huapi*, Anales de Parques Nacionales, XIV:7-43. Buenos Aires, 1978.

Pérez Rosales, Vicente. *Recuerdos del pasado*. Buenos Aires, 1944.

Porcel de Peralta, Manuel. *Biografía de Nahuel Huapi*, second edition. S.C. de Bariloche, 1959.

Racedo, Eduardo. *La conquista del desierto*. Buenos Aires, 1881.

Ramayón, Eduardo E. *Nahuel Huapi. Campaña militar 1881*. Buenos Aires, 1936.

Ramos Mejía, Ezequiel. *Mis memorias, 1853-1935*. Buenos Aires, 1936.

Raone, Juan Mario. *Fortines del desierto*. Buenos Aires, 1969.

Ruiz Moreno, Isidoro. *En Nahuel Huapi con Theodore Roosevelt en 1913*, Anales de Parques Nacionales, III:125-130. Buenos Aires, 1953.

Schoo Lastra, Dionisio. *El indio del desierto, 1535-1879*. Buenos Aires, 1928.

Steffen, Juan. *Westpatagonien. Die patagonischen Kordilleren und ihre Randgebiete*. Berlin, 1919.

Steffen, Juan. *Dr. Franz Foncks Lebensgang und wissenschaftliche Bedeutung*. Santiago, 1913.

Varela, Luis V. *La República Argentina y Chile. Historia de la demarcación de sus fronteras, 1843-1899*. Buenos Aires, 1899.

Verniory, G. *Diez años en la Araucanía, 1889-1899.* Santiago, 1975.

Vignati, Milcíades A. *El asiento de la misión jesuítica del lago Nahuel Huapi,* Boletín de la Junta de Historia y Numismática, VIII:315-321. Buenos Aires, 1936.

Vignati, Milcíades A. *Iconografía aborigen. Los caciques Sayhueque, Inacayal, Foyel y sus allegados,* Revista del Museo de la Plata, II:13-48. La Plata, 1943.

Villegas, Conrado E. *Expedición al gran lago Nahuel Huapi en 1887,* second edition. Buenos Aires, 1974.

Walter, J. C. *La conquista del desierto: síntesis histórica de los principales sucesos ocurridos y operaciones militares realizadas en la Pampa y Patagonia contra los indios (1527-1885),* third edition. Buenos Aires, 1970.

Williams, Glyn. *The Desert and the Dream. A Study of Welsh Colonization in Chubut 1865-1915.* University of Wales Press. Cardiff, 1975.

Willis, Bayley. *Northern Patagonia.* New York, 1914.

Ygobone, Aquiles D. *Francisco P. Moreno, precursor de la Patagonia.* Buenos Aires, 1952.

Zeballos, Estanislao. *Demarcación de límites entre la República Argentina y Chile.* Buenos Aires, 1892.

Zeballos, Estanislao. *La conquista de quince mil leguas.* Buenos Aires, 1878.

This first edition is limited to 2000 numbered
copies in Spanish and 1000 numbered copies
in English, and was printed on November 30th
1989 at Gaglianone Establecimiento Gráfico
S.A., Chilavert 1146, Buenos Aires, Argentina.

2698